THE BEAUT.IE

THE
beaut.ie
GUIDE TO
gorgeous

AISLING MCDERMOTT

GILL & MACMILLAN

Gill & Macmillan Ltd

Hume Avenue, Park West, Dublin 12

with associated companies throughout the world

www.gillmacmillan.ie

© Aisling McDermott 2009

978 07171 4590 4

Design by Design Image, Dublin

Illustrations © Olivia Golden

Printed and bound by Grafo, Spain

This book is typeset in 11pt Crono MM on 19pt leading.

LIBRARIES NI	
C700248953	
RONDO	24/02/2010
646.72	£ 15.50
RTC	

A CIP catalogue record for this book is available from the British Library.

ACKNOWLEDGMENTS

So many people helped me in the writing of this book and I want to say a great big thanks to them all. So, in no particular order:

Donal Costigan, who has inspired me with his can-do attitude and kept me going when others would have given up. Without him, I would quite literally not have been able to do any of this.

Róisín Ingle, who always sees the potential in people and had the idea for the book in the first place. At first it was all a bit, 'Hey, let's put on the show right here in the barn!', but in about half an hour I was seeing my way to how it might happen, and after one appletini too many I was convinced she had had another of her great ideas.

The lovely Faith O'Grady at the Lisa Richards Agency, whose tenacity and, er, faith in me were tireless. If she believes in you, that keeps you going like a Duracell Bunny.

My sister, Kirstie McDermott, who is a font of knowledge about the cosmetics industry and who dreamed up the Beaut.ie blog. She is a total superstar and gave me lots of help when writing this.

Sarah Liddy at Gill & Macmillan, who spotted the blog's potential to become a book and gave me the best trip to publication anyone could ever have.

All the Beaut.ies who log on every day, comment, enter our competitions and make blogging so much damn fun – you're the reason we do this.

My wonderful family: Mum, Dad and Shauna.

And most of all to Derrick. You know why.

INTRODUCTION
Confessions of a Product Junkie

My sister Kirstie and I always spent all our pocket money on skincare, make-up and magazines. Along with copies of *Jackie*, we bought Clearasil and mud masks in sachets. *Just Seventeen* was accompanied by Rimmel Hide the Blemish and Black Cherry lipstick. Yes, in our teenage years we were obsessed with spots and make-up. We got perms, we grew them out, we tried every new and disgusting make-up on the market and cleansers so strong they made our eyes water. Hint of a Tint and sachets of henna ruined every bathroom towel Beaut.ie mammy ever bought. Once something was cheap and full of promise, it claimed its place on the bathroom shelves.

By our twenties, we'd moved on to *Marie Claire*, *Cosmo*, Clinique and Lancôme. When a new ad came on the telly for something that looked fabulous, it was ours. When I moved out of the family home, my sisters said the thing they missed most about me were all the beauty products I took with me. Charming.

Blogging Is the Best Fun You Can Have with Your Clothes On

Nowadays we read beauty blogs and go for all the latest salon treatments. Brown Thomas's Beauty Hall is a temple of worship and I'm ashamed to admit that we can blow a fair bit of cash in there. When Kirstie suggested we set up our very own beauty blog, it seemed like a logical extension. After all, there was nothing out there for Irish gals and we had plenty of experiences to write about. So Beaut.ie came to be, out of love, out of an enduring fascination with the subject and out of a sense of fun. And people started to read! Eventually tens of thousands of people started to log on. They left comments and the things they said were hilarious! We were hooked. We became addicted to blogging and we loved Beaut.ie like nothing else we'd ever done.

The Book Was Born

Along the way, we've picked up quite a bit of knowledge. We try out everything new on the market and know exactly what works and what doesn't. But one thing remains true: Beaut.ie is irreverent and doesn't take itself seriously at all. From the get-go, we understood that people want to know what actually works before they splash out on it. And they want to know what other people think about it. Beaut.ie was perfect for this – we could give our opinions and other people could pitch in with their thoughts.

I want you to use this book in the same spirit. Go straight to the chapters that you're interested in – or read the whole way through. Beauty is meant to be enjoyable. Don't ever worry about looking like a supermodel – that's their *job*. You're a real person and you want to find skincare that works and foundation that actually suits you. This book will help you and so will the advice and experiences of all the people who have contributed to it.

Above all, have fun. Channel your inner Lovely Girl, dress her up in a nice frock and take her out somewhere special. She likes cocktails.

1

Wash it Off

LIKE FOUNDATION, THE SEARCH FOR THE PERFECT CLEANSER IS A GRAIL QUEST...

WHAT TYPE ARE YOU THEN?

Babaduck
It used to be very dry and flaky in my 20s but has become oilier. Shiny forehead, oily but flaky nose, dry cheeks and oily chin.

Nicki
I have normal skin but sometimes suffer from dry flaky patches on my nose and under the eyes, which looks awful when I put make-up on. I use Origins Never A Dull Moment exfoliator every second day and it's brilliant, it really works! Eight Hour Cream is a lifesaver for dry patches, what would we do without Lizzie?

CarolineJ
My Ultra Bland from Lush is working a treat. Think it's my Eve Lom muslin cloth in the warm shower, my skin isn't congested, feels clear and no dry patches at all.

Surely we all know what skintype we have. Don't we all slot neatly into a little position on the skintype scale and scurry off to buy perfectly formulated products for said type?

Not at all. I'd say no two of us have skin that behaves perfectly to type. A lot of us have skin that's a little bit of one type and a little bit of another. You can suffer from dehydration with almost any skintype and congestion can hit us all at one stage or another. So I wouldn't worry too much about having a skin 'type' and trying to squash yourself into a category. It isn't a cut-and-dried issue at all. I can't tell you how many therapists I've seen who've told me completely different things about my skin. Through trial and error and finding out more about it, I've realised that they were probably all right – even though they told me different things. How can this be?

Well, skin reacts to ageing, the weather, the seasons, the type of products you're using on it and stress, and as a result, your skintype may vary. So that's why you won't find a category for 'normal' in this chapter, because I've never come across a person who has perfectly behaved skin 100 per cent of the time. Everyone has some area of concern.

In the heel of the hunt, I discovered that my skin is normal/combination with a strong tendency towards dehydration and becomes very congested in the T-zone.

But what the hell does that all mean? It means that like most of us, I need to chop and change my skincare routine slightly, depending on how things are looking.

But doesn't that cost a fortune? Not really, because I didn't rush out and buy everything at once. Products last for ages and ages if you're only using a small bit of them or only using them now and again. But do always check the expiry date on the pot. Plus, of course, there are great ranges to suit every pocket, so you don't have to spend loads if you don't want to. And if in doubt, it's time to treat yourself to one of the greatest pleasures there is – a facial, of course – so that you can consult with the experts.

TAKE IT ALL OFF WITH A MUSLIN CLOTH

A lot of high-end brands use a muslin cloth as an integral part of their cleansing routine, and here's a tip: a muslin cloth will enhance the performance of any cleanser. From something that you carefully selected in a salon to Aldi's finest, try taking it off with a muslin cloth. Using a cloth every time you cleanse will gently exfoliate and deep cleanse the skin, and boost circulation while it's at it.

Laura F

I think it is combination-sensitive, oily in the T-zone and dry on my cheeks. I'm using a mixture of different products at the moment. Think I found my Holy Grail Cleanser, the Origins White Tea cleanser. It's just gorgeous, leaves my face so soft. Still love the Clarins Pure Melt for make-up removal though as well!

ams

There is a Boots Balm cleanser which is quite nice and it comes with two muslin cloths. It's from the Time Delay range.

Bee

Body Shop does muslin face cloths in packs of three if you want to try those. They're not as soft as the Liz Earle ones, but I think they're grand. I still have mine and also one from Eve Lom. Molton Brown also does a cleanser with a muslin cloth, so that could be an option too.

THE QUEST FOR PERFECTION

Like foundation, the search for the perfect cleanser is a Grail Quest. It's really important to get this vital step right. To use a corny expression, it's the cornerstone of any beauty routine. I firmly believe that this is the building block your whole beauty routine should be based on, so it's vital to find a routine which suits you, because when it does, your skin will glow and feel great.

Of course, your cleanser depends on your individual preference: do you like foaming cleansers, gel, washes, milk, oil or cream? But first things first. Let's discuss what you shouldn't use – The Wipe.

WORK OF SATAN: Make-up Wipes

We're always giving out about these yokes on Beaut.ie. All a make-up wipe will do – no matter how fancy-pants it seems – is wipe the top layer of make-up off. It won't clean down into the pores or actually cleanse your face properly at all. Use a make-up wipe – any brand – regularly, and your skin will start to look dull and clogged up. Areas of congestion and blackheads will follow, mark my words.

Gingerrama
You can also use wipes for household cleaning. OK, maybe not a whole house, but fine for small jobs in a small flat.

And if the wipe tells you it can do four things at once – cleanse, tone, moisturise and hang out the washing, for example – beware. How can one product do all these things effectively?

Look, I'm realistic. I know we've all got a packet of make-up wipes in the drawer beside the bed. The only time it's acceptable to use these things is at half two in the morning when you've stumbled home after a night on the razzle. Before you fall into bed, you might use one of these to forestall the dreaded Shroud of Turin effect on your pillow the next morning.

Sadly, though, make-up wipes are the best-selling cleanser in Ireland. Supermarket shelves positively groan with them, which is probably why they're so popular. They're handy to throw in your trolley as you pass and think you've got your cleansing sorted. You haven't, though. Make a new resolution to give them up this year. You can do it.

Lynnie

I used to exclusively use wipes to cleanse. Then I went for my first facial and my therapist nearly cried when I told her. She said she didn't give a toss what brand I used as long as I got myself a proper cleanser – and my skin improved nearly immediately.

CLEANSERS FOR YOUNG SKIN

Ah, teenage skin, I remember you well. What I remember most about you is the spots that erupted every time there was an evint of the utmost social importance, like a GAA disco (or horrors – the No Name Club). All the early teenage me had to disguise a nuclear-looking zit was some Sudocrem – and in moments of utter despair, I would put talc atop the Sudocrem.

I would burn the life out of those spots and scrub my face with Biactol and Clearasil. Skincare was like firefighting: I would viciously attack any sign of an outbreak with the skin equivalent of fire foam. Facemasks for me were the sort you made out of pots of natural yoghurt or whatever was recommended in *Just Seventeen* that week. Once it came in a sachet and thus cost no more than 50p, it was good enough for me.

Listen, times weren't easy. Not only was I grappling with monster blackheads on my nose, I was struggling with hated homework and having a million unrequited crushes on any half-decent boy that strayed into my path. Plus I could *never* get my hair to do that flicky thing I wanted it to so badly.

But times have thankfully changed. The beauty industry has realised that the strongest force teenage skin has to fight is hormonal and have changed their products accordingly. The ranges that are around now are much more balanced and soothing. And since the second-strongest force teenage skin must contend with is lack of money, there are plenty of inexpensive options out there.

If you have a more serious skincare issue, like acne, fear not. The doctor or the dermatologist will be able to sort you out and they should be your first port of call. Get Mammy to bring you – and pay for you.

Great Picks for Young Skin
Neutrogena Wave

Your friend for effective, deep cleansing will be a handy little motorised doofer, the Neutrogena Wave. You attach a product-infused cleansing pad, switch it on and away you go – skin is deep-cleaned in a jiffy.

Vichy Young Skin Set

It can be really difficult to get good products for problem skin that aren't horrid and harsh, so that's why I like Vichy's Young Skin Set range, designed for ages 16 to 20. It receives rave reviews and that's because of its abilities to regulate skin that's going mintil due to hormonal changes.

Supermarket Sweeps

Avoid anything heavily perfumed and alcohol-packed and instead look for cleansers from brands like Simple and Neutrogena. Less is more with your skintype, as you just need a good cleanser with no frills. Try Neutrogena's Visibly Clear 2-in-1 Wash and Mask on a daily basis to keep blemishes in check, or throw Simple's Oil Balancing Exfoliating Wash into your basket next time you're doing the shopping.

Facial Focus

Check out Dermalogica. Not only is it a great brand for anyone experiencing skin issues, men get on great with it too. They've expanded the range in recent years and there's now a targeted line, Anti-Bac, for problem skins. If you're at your wit's end with your skin, there are Dermalogica salons all over Ireland where you can get targeted treatments as well as pro advice on at-home products. Hurray! Also reccomended: Nelsons Pure & Clear range, Dermalogica Medibac Overnight Clearing Gel and Murad Vitamin C Environmental Shield Facial.

Spots

For serious acne problems, I recommend that you visit your GP or a dermatologist. There's so much they can do to help, so don't suffer in silence. Topical treatments like cleansers and spot creams can only do so much – if they're not working for you, it's time to go to the experts.

For people with acne scarring, a course of IPL (intense pulsed light) carried out by a dermatologist can have great results.

Gingerrama

I've used it – not all over, just on spots and spottier areas. I've used it as a teenager, so that would be about 20 years ago. Dries out spots nicely. It's a teeny bit of a palaver, but nothing drastic. Not a good idea to use all over, unless your skin is actually oilier, tougher and zittier all over. And avoid the eye, corner of nose and lip area.

Ellenwaxer

As a paste, this is excellent on ingrown hairs, as it's basically the same stuff that's in Tend Skin or Vanish. Obviously not suitable for those allergic to asprin, pregnant or with further contraindications.

Nikki

I find that taking zinc and vitamin C helps with skin breakouts lately. Big difference to me, finally skin not too bad. It's great! I'd touch wood if I had some 'touch virtual wood'!

DIY: Aspirin Facemask

Never mind Sudocrem – a lot of people put crushed-up aspirin tablets on their spots and it does seem to work. Why? Well, aspirin contains, amongst other things, acetasalicylic acid.

Chemically, this is like salicylic acid, which is an ingredient widely used by the cosmetic industry to clear skin and dry up spots. Plus it seems to bring down inflammation, even when applied topically (straight onto the skin for you and me, as opposed to swallowed).

It can be used as a facemask and exfoliator for anyone with oily/acne prone/congested skin. Here's what you need:

- 4 aspirin tablets
- 1 tablespoon of water
- oil or honey

1. Dissolve the aspirin in the water and mix in a little oil (whichever oil you like best – olive oil is fine) or honey. You need these to help the mask stick to your face and to stop it from getting powdery.
2. Apply a thin layer of the paste to your face, paying particular attention to spot-prone or congested areas.
3. Leave on for 10 minutes. Rub the mask gently into pores when you're removing it and it does a great job of exfoliating too.

PRODUCT OF YORE: Sudocrem

The chances are you've been acquainted with it since day one. A staple in every family bathroom cabinet, it's used, of course, for nappy rash. In teenage years, it again proved its worth as our favourite spot cream. It's humble, it's not encased in fancy packaging (far from it) and there's no swanky advertising campaigns, but we love it 'cos it works to dry up those nasty spots and it's kept on working for generations. Mammy recommends.

Top Tip: If you're getting an onslaught of spots or other forms of congestion, you could be using too much moisturiser and overloading your skin. Try cutting down and see if this helps.

Top Tip: Getting spots around your mouth? Throw out any lip glosses/lip balms that could be harbouring bacteria. Clean your phone mouthpieces with antibacterial wipes and make sure you clean your make-up brushes properly.

CoffeeSusan
The space between my eyebrows is looking like something the armed garda response unit would be using for target practice. I suspect that this is an area that I'm managing to miss a little when exfoliating, as I'm concentrating on not getting anything in my eyes.

GREEN AND GORGEOUS: Tea Tree Oil

FilthyCute
I use concentrated tea tree oil in a basin of hot water to wash my face with after cleansing. I think it's fab, and you can get it in Boots etc. for dirt cheap. Five drops in the basin and you're grand, then put a dab on a cotton bud and onto a spot if it needs it.

Krista
I bought a tea tree oil blemish stick at The Body Shop the other day, and I think it might actually be doing the trick. My hormonally induced chin spot is dying far more quickly than it ever has.

Cleansers for Oily Skin

It's not just younger skin that tends to be oily, and you'll need to use specially formulated products, of which there are some good 'uns. It's most common for adult oily skin to be concentrated around the T-zone area, and if this is the case, you have combination skin – you'll probably find the skin on your cheeks is completely different. Wash your face twice a day with a refreshing gel cleanser – no more, or you run the risk of actually causing your skin to produce more sebum as it struggles to compensate; see the over-cleansing advice on p. 16.

Great Picks for Oily Skin
Vichy Normaderm Deep Cleansing Gel

Vichy Normaderm Deep Cleansing Gel is great for oily and congestion-prone skin and is an absolute stand-out cleanser for anyone with these issues. Use this green gel for a couple of weeks and you'll find a huge difference in your skin. It works like a particularly effective drain un-blocker on your blackheads and seems to stop spots in their tracks too. Skin is left smoother, with noticeably fewer blackheads and outbreaks. An inexpensive star product that is available from every chemist, it's a wonder-cleanser for oily, congested, combination or skin prone to zits. Plus, there's a whole Normaderm range of complimentary and equally effective products.

NeoStrata Foaming Glycolic Wash

If you're serious about getting super-smooth, oil-controlled skin, then a glycolic wash like NeoStrata's Foaming Glycolic Wash will be right up your street. This product works and then some. Don't plan any hot dates while you're in the middle of your glycolic experience, though. You will probably break out like never before as your skin struggles to clear itself. All that gunk has to go somewhere. You'll also get really dry skin which will eventually flake off. (The attractive Lizard Look.)

This does all sound a bit gross, I know, but boy, will you look amazing after a few weeks. Hold your nerve and make sure to wear a rich moisturiser and an effective sunblock.

Shu Uemura High

Shu Uemura's High Performance Balancing Cleansing Oil Fresh was developed for oily, combination and acne-prone skin – in other words, for anyone who longed to use their regular cleansing oil but felt it was too rich for them. In my drive to get the whole world to experience the joy of using cleansing oil, I urge you to give it a try. Like the regular High Performance Balancing Cleansing Oil, this will lift off a whole face of make-up in a trice. Fresh goes further, though – it also contains cherry extract to gently exfoliate and lift impurities and will leave your skin refreshed and calm.

Facial Focus

When you want a bit of pampering or extra help, look for a facial that's purifying – this is exactly what your skintype likes. Book yourself in for a Matis Purifying treatment quick-smart. Widely available around the country, this will decongest problem areas and help to balance acidity, so it won't go

Deirdre

I find that using NeoStrata Foaming Glycolic Wash is a great upkeep in between glycolic peels. I use it twice a day and use Soap & Glory Scrub Your Nose In It scrub/mask every second day. My skin hasn't looked this good in ages. I think the combo of the chemical peel effect with the NeoStrata wash and the physical grainy scrub of the Soap & Glory is what's doing it. The glycolic loosens the dead skin and the scrub scrubs it off. Don't know how I lived before glycolic acid …

Nikki

Girls, have to tell you about my recent success with the Effaclar range from La Roche-Posay, finding it fantastic for oily skin. Using a mousse foam wash cleanser, toner and matte moisturising fluid! My skin hasn't been this good in ages – doesn't break the bank either.

Zoulikha

La Roche-Posay Physiological one is perfect for me. Tried nearly everything on the market for oily-breakout skin. This is the best for me.

gloss

I love Dermalogica's beauty cleansing bar (it's a bar of non-soap soap). I've got combination skin and it takes everything off, but it's still very gentle on your skin. It sounds expensive, but it lasts forever – cut it into three blocks with a knife! It's also fantastic for travelling; you get to bring a little piece of it instead of a big bottle of cleanser.

zee

Bioré do a few pore unclogging and blackhead-busting face washes that I find give the same results as Dermalogica, but for a fair whack less money.

so mad on sebum overload. Also recommended: Matis Purifying Gel, Yes to Tomatoes Trouble-free Facial Wash and Yonka Le Grand Classique Facial.

Over-cleansing

Once people get really enthusiastic about a cleansing routine, I've noticed that they can sometimes start to cleanse too much. If cleanliness is next to godliness, why not get super clean? Those of us with oily or spot-prone skin might think that the best way to tackle any problems is to cleanse morning, noon and night and keep any dirt and grime firmly at bay.

But it doesn't work quite like that. Repeated cleansing of the skin, especially with heavy-duty cleansers, strips the skin of sebum, which it can then work hard to regenerate, leading to – yes, you've guessed it – yet more oiliness and spots. I've heard loads of horror stories from folks who have used the wrong products for their skin, leading to horrendous breakouts. If your skin starts to overreact, stop using any new products – they're probably too harsh for you. Quite often, skin only needs a proper cleanse at night-time to get rid of the grime of the day. Try cleansing thoroughly at night and just using a splash of water (you can wipe over some rosewater) in the morning and see how you get on. If you've got oily skin, you might like to use a mild cleanser instead, but don't overdo it.

Top Tip: A professional extraction during a facial is the business. The beautician will squeeze every one of those yucky blackheads out of your nose/chin/forehead. A bit uncomfortable – but oh, so worth it!

AREAS OF CONGESTION

Areas of congestion, blackheads, whiteheads, pimples – whatever you call them – they're gunk that clogs up skin and are really difficult to clear up. A great facial with extractions is a brilliant place to start, but how do you keep everything clear? Use a fab product that takes no prisoners in the battle against blackheads but is gentle enough not to ravage skin. Glycolic washes like NeoStrata are fantastic for this. And of course, if you want to win the battle completely, go for a course of glycolic peels. A fantastic treatment, it got rid of my areas of congestion once and for all.

JustMe

I found the Magic Mitt by Jane Iredale. It's fab and leaves you squeaky clean, not a trace of make-up and all you need to do is wet it. My skin has never been so good! I throw it in the washing machine once a week for a complete full-on clean.

I have skin that plays up and I have found it has really cleared up. Bacteria does not seem to attach itself and I'm sure I have saved loads of money also.

Cow Love

I had a facial a few weeks ago in Galway and they did extractions! My god I thought she was going to break my nose and I couldn't breathe as she was holding both my nostrils closed! Apart from that it was fab, though, and my skin has been great since!

Seal

Toleriane is recommended for sensitive eyes/contact lens wearers and I've often found that when eye make-up removers are advertised this way they are basically repackaged water and completely ineffective at removing make-up.

Toleriane (without wanting to sound over-dramatic!) is definitely the exception to the rule. Two words: IT WORKS. A great product, this cleanser would suit anybody, not just those with sensitive eyes.

Kathryn

I keep going back to this product, I have SUPER-sensitive eyes and have tried every bloody product ever, but this not only doesn't affect my eyes, it works!

EYE MAKE-UP REMOVERS
La Roche-Posay Toleriane

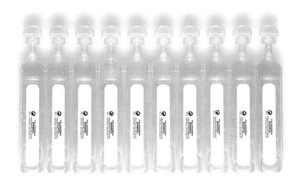

So pure you don't even need to wash it off. Formulated for those with super-sensitive eyes and contact lens wearers, this won't irritate. We've also found those single-use capsules very handy for weekends away when you don't want to be carting a whole bottle of eye make-up remover with you.

Clinique Take the Day Off

Make-up is powerless before this stuff. Long-wear lipsticks and waterproof mascara melt away, and all traces of shadow and liner will be wiped away with one fell swoop. Brillo.

PRODUCT OF YORE: Anne French

There isn't a woman in the land who hasn't possessed a bottle of this milky substance. We loved it as teenage Beaut.ies, but as far as we can remember, it delivered absolutely no benefits whatsoever. We think it might be because the rest of the world had forgotten us and we had about two products we were able to buy in Ireland, so we all bought them. Collective consciousness, how are ya?

Like most Products of Yore, the manufacturers ain't letting this one go. It should have been left behind in the 1980s, but it's with us today and that means people are still buying it. The packaging has been tarted up, but that's about it.

CLEANSERS FOR DRY SKIN

Rule number one for dry skintypes: stay away from foaming or face wash cleansers if you have dry or sensitive skin.

Go for cleansers that will actually moisturise your skin while they wipe away all the dirt and make-up. Cleansing lotions with a creamy texture will be kind to you. Bear in mind that your skin changes with the seasons as well as with the years, and adjust your cleanser to cope with this. What suited you down to the ground in your twenties is unlikely to cut the mustard in your thirties.

Great Picks for Dry Skin
Balms

Solid balm-type cleansers and oils are ideal for make-up removal and cleansing. Finding a good product for dry skin is so important – the difference it makes is incredible – so don't feel guilty about spending a little extra. Try one of these.

Hot Cloth Cleansing

Liz Earle Cleanse & Polish Hot Cloth Cleanser and Eve Lom Cleanser are constantly rated by us and by the Beaut.ies. So deserving of praise, they're getting their own panel where I gush about their brilliance.

Clinique Take the Day Off Cleansing Balm

A solid balm you rub into make-up, this is a staple at every Clinique counter the land over, so it's easy to find and not extortionately priced.

Lush Ultra Bland

I know it's not a very awe-inspiring name, but what it lacks in witty monikers it makes up for in cleansing terms – rich and waxy, it's packed full of oils and honey, making it brillo for 'normal' and dry skins. Just hold your nose when you go into Lush to buy it.

EVE LOM OR LIZ EARLE?

I can wax lyrical about cleanser all day. Eve Lom Cleanser and Liz Earle Cleanse & Polish Hot Cloth are both famous for good reason. These two standout cleansers are always mentioned in tandem whenever we have a discussion on Beaut.ie about which cleanser is the absolute best ever. Both are multi-award-winners and come from brilliant ranges. Both use a muslin cloth method and are packed full of scrumptious ingredients. So how do you decide which one to go for?

Eve Lom is a thick, waxy, balm-type cleanser, while Liz Earle has a rich, creamy formulation that smells fresh. Price tends to be the higgest consideration between the two, though. There's no doubt about it that Eve Lom is expensive (with a capital E). It's the Crème de la Mer of cleansers, but if you're a luxury freak and you have the readies to spend, then go for Eve Lom.

If you want high quality, high performance, fresh botanicals, a more reasonable price and a cleanser that consistently wins beauty awards too, then get the Liz Earle version.

Or do what I did and try them both. Ask for Eve for a present and buy Liz yourself.

girlfriday
Lush Ultra Bland cleanser is fab. Have always been a big fan of oil/balm-type cleansers, and even if using a milk cleanser, I always use the auld hot washcloth/muslin cloth to remove. Molton Brown Softcleanse Rosewax Liquefier is also gorgeous.

Gracie
As a cheap alternative to Eve Lom, Boots do something similar. It's their Time Delay range. It's a balm you massage onto dry skin and remove with damp muslin cloths that are provided. Have used it on and off over the last seven years and my skin is always radiant when using it.

Alethea

I am a huge fan of cleansing lotions as I have extremely dry skin, and find they are much gentler on my skin than other types of cleansers. I find the Weleda Wild Rose Cleanser brilliant – it leaves my skin so soft, it smells of roses, it contains rosehip oil (so you get the benefit of oils) and it only costs approx. 11 euro! Definitely a good choice if your skin is dry and flaky like mine.

Babaduck

I hate anything that's applied with cotton wool, as to me it never leaves my skin feeling clean enough. I used to use Clinique's Comforting Cream Cleanser, but have switched to the Lancôme Baume Éclat and I absolutely lurve it with all my heart. I much prefer using a facecloth and water to cleanse and this is a perfect companion.

L'Argent

I am also a huge fan of Liz Earle Cleanse & Polish and I also think Lush's Angels on Bare Skin is great!

Pooch

For those of you feeling guilty regarding the price of Eve Lom, this cleanser is honestly FOUR PRODUCTS rolled into one – cleanser, toner, eye make-up remover and exfoliator.

Speccy

Liz Earle – no need to try anything else. Love the smell, the texture, the hot cloth feeling – clean but not too functional. Skin stays in great condition.

By The Hokey:

In the 1920s, an innovative product was invented by a fella called Leo Gerstenzang in New York. His company marketed baby care accessories and these little sticks of wood topped with cotton were used to clean baby's ears after a bath. Hilariously to us now, they were first called Baby Gays. You can see the reasoning – they were for babies and they made said babies happy because their ears were clean. Hence, Baby Gays. Leo made the name even more fancy a few years later and changed it to Quality-tips Baby Gays.

For obvious reasons, the whole Baby Gay part of the name was dropped. Perhaps people felt uncomfortable cleaning out their earwax or putting on eyeshadow with a Baby Gay? (I can't believe that anyone *does* put on eyeshadow with one of these, but apparently it's not unheard of.)

Unilever owns Baby Gays now and they call them Q-tips. They sell a mind-boggling 25.5 billion of these things a year.

AISLING'S PICK

Shu Uemura cleansing oils are the absolute cat's pyjamas when it comes to make-up removal and super-cleansing all in one. All you do is pump a couple of squirts of oil out into your hand, rub it into your face and add water. The oil emulsifies and goes milky, and when you rinse, your whole faceful of make-up will be heading drain-wards.

Just as quick as a wipe but about a hundred times more effective, Asian women swear by these cleansers and I can testify to the fact that they are fabilis. They used to be tricky to get a hold of, as only high-end brands like Shu Uemura produced them, but when more mainstream brands like Lancôme and Clarins jumped on the bandwagon, they made oil cleansers more easily available – and cheaper.

As an added bonus, the oils are very moisturising and leave your skin soft and silky. If cleansers normally leave your skin feeling a little bit tight and dry, then it's time to give cleansing oils a go.

UnaSpoona

I use Tesco Vitamin E Cleansing Lotion and it's great! Cheap as chips but gets the job done. I'm mid-30s with fairly problem-free skin. Sometimes it can be dry and I don't wear tons of make-up, so I don't need a heavy-duty cleanser.

Aisling

Cetaphil is brilliant but its packaging is completely off-putting – you'd mistake it for a bathroom cleaner instead of anything you would put on your face. I found out about it the last time I went to the States – the guy sitting beside me on the flight was telling me about a list of things he had been asked to bring back to his girlfriend, and this was top of the list. Curiosity got the better of me, and I had to try it.

girlfriday

I totally agree with the fabulousness of cleansing oils, and the Shu Uemura range. Fantastic stuff, really melts all the gunk you manage to collect on your face during the day and leaves you feeling clean and soft and fabulous.

EcoBabe

I use a lovely Irish organic brand, Nádúr Organics Pure Cleanse Facial Oil, which is fab and the amount of dirt that comes out of my pores is just pure frightening!

minxinparis

Love this product. Started off with the original oil about 30 years ago, now use the one for sensitive skin. It takes off everything, even my Lancôme waterproof mascara, so easy-peasy to use and leaves your skin feeling supple rather than taut. I have allergies and eczema but no probs with this product.

Good substitute is the new Clarins Pure Melt Cleansing Gel.

Kirstie

This is my make-up removal product of absolute choice! It just melts it away, like magic. Lancôme's Huile Clarte and Chanel's cleansing oil are both good alternatives and are much easier to get. Neither of them is as superb at cutting through a face full of make-up, but if you'd never used Shu, you'd still be delighted at the result.

DIY: Make Your Own Cleansing Oil

Before I tell you this grubby story, I'll add a disclaimer: I've never tried it and I never will. Specially formulated cleansing oils are not cooking oils. They contain emulsifiers and other ingredients that make them work well to cleanse and purify. It's no easy matter getting this mix right – which is why Shu Uemura are the best in the business. But because people are agog to know about this DIY cleanser, I'll share the greasy secret.

This subject provoked an unprecedented amount of commentary and discussion on Beaut.ie that continued enthusiastically for weeks. And months. Everyone had an opinion, and if they didn't, they wanted to know more.

Beaut.ie Lynnie was a convert at first and told us, 'If you don't believe me, ask reader Pixie, who has very oily skin and swears by it.' Sez she: 'After about three weeks, my blackheads started to fall out and now I rarely have any breakouts or flaky episodes. People have asked me did I go to a dermatologist because there has been such an improvement.' Princess Buttercup had a similar blackhead-busting experience: 'Yup, they fell out of their own disgusting accord.'

You need a mix of castor oil and another (secondary) oil like extra virgin olive oil, hemp oil, jojoba oil, monoi oil or sunflower seed oil. Pick any one of these oils you prefer. Real experts go for the jojoba oil, but go ahead and use the Tesco sunflower oil if you like.) Don't use pure castor oil – it's drying, so that's why you need to mix it with another.

- **Oily skin:** 30 per cent castor oil and 70 per cent secondary oil.
- **Normal skin:** 20 per cent castor oil and 80 per cent secondary oil.
- **Dry skin:** 10 per cent castor oil and 90 per cent secondary oil.
- A drop of aromatherapy oil will stop you from smelling like the chipper.

When it was revealed that castor oil was a natural emulsifier and could be used in homemade cleansing oil, it sold out of chemists across the country. But this caused some confusion amongst our pharmacists, who thought everyone was trying to buy laxatives.

But even as the experiment progressed and it seemed as though half the women in the country were trying out this DIY method, the tales of joy

Roseyrosie
Is it sunflower oil, like for cooking with? Or do you have to get organic stuff? I'm not planning on using Crisp 'n Dry but thought I'd check!

Little Blue
I've been trying to buy castor oil since reading Pixie's original post during the week. I've tried a few small chemists in my town. I've got everything from 'nobody sells that any more, it's been banned' to 'we could order it in for you but it comes in a 5-litre bottle' and my favourite, 'have you tried Senokot?'

Felicia
I've been aching to try out this oil cleansing method, but I've been to three different pharmacies and I am still unable to find any of this elusive castor oil. I've searched high and low at the 'laxative' section, and even tried supermarkets, to no avail.

turned into less euphoric reports. Turns out castor oil is not a very effective emulsifier. Spots and angry outbreaks were woefully described. My advice? Stick to a proper manufactured cleansing oil.

CLEANSERS FOR SENSITIVE AND ROSACEA-PRONE SKIN

With over 50 per cent of women claiming to suffer from sensitive skin (figures vary depending on who's had the research commissioned), it's clear that this is an issue that an awful lot of you find problematic. Our Irish skin is practically pre-programmed to be sensitive and rosacea-prone, so it's important that we find good-quality products that don't irritate. Milk and fluid cleansers are particularly good for this sort of skin, as they help to keep it calm during the cleansing process.

Practically every skincare brand now has a 'sensitive' side, but which ones are actually any good? Look for ranges where harsh ingredients have been swapped with gentler ones, perfumes are removed and milder formulations achieved. It's now possible to combine any skintype with a sensitive formula and get results. Here are the ones that really work.

Deb

I have rosacea and very sensitive skin and La Roche-Posay Toleriane cleanser/moisturiser along with the Thermal Spa Water is excellent.

Great Picks for Sensitive Skin
La Roche-Posay Toleraine

I'm a huge fan of pretty much every La Roche-Posay product ever invented, and their Toleriane cleanser is no different. A calming product that's purer than water, it's my number-one recommendation for sensitive skin.

RoC Calmance Soothing Cleansing Fluid

RoC Calmance Soothing Cleansing Fluid is widely available and is especially good for redness sufferers. It's a no-rinse product so you can avoid any irritation caused by water – a common complaint for sensitive types.

Aveeno Ultra-Calming Foaming Cleanser

Aveeno Ultra-Calming Foaming Cleanser contains the magic ingredient feverfew, which works to calm prickly skin. Dermatologists rate this stuff, as it's so kind to use. Even if you find that nothing else works, this should do the trick.

Dermalogica Ultracalming Cleanser

Tons of Beaut.ies love Dermalogica Ultracalming Cleanser. It's a highly rated salon cleanser for sensitive skin, much loved by our readers because of its ability to effectively clean delicate skin without causing massive upset.

Top Tip: If your skin is reacting and so sensitive that even water irritates it, try cleansing with milk for a few days to calm it down.

Top Tip: Look out for anything containing feverfew as an ingredient, as it's anti-inflammatory and superbly calming. RoC and Aveeno incorporate it into some of their products.

EXFOLIATION

This is a must. Exfoliation involves getting rid of dead skin cells to reveal a fresher, brighter layer of skin. And sure, that makes you look younger. Try to use your exfoliator a maximum of three times a week — any more could harm your skin.

Exfoliation is absolutely necessary for a clear, glowing complexion. Used on a regular basis, it will go a long way to stopping blackheads rearing their ugly, er, heads and it will make your moisturiser and sunscreen work better too.

As well as your regular cleansing regime, it does your skin good to have a deep-down clean on a regular basis. Even if you've got dry skin, a gentle exfoliant will do wonders for your skin by lifting away dead skin cells. Just don't scrub.

There are three main types: manual, chemical and enzymatic, and the one you'll encounter most at home will be the manual variety, as it's the one where you scrub little beads across your face to slough off dead skin cells and tackle congestion. But there are just so many of them out there. How do you know what to use?

Great Picks for Exfoliation
Dr LeWinns Facial Polishing Gel

Lots of people love a scrub that feels really rough against their skin — so they can be assured that it's working, like. But I'd avoid a scrub that almost hurts. Try Dr LeWinns pineappley Facial Polishing Gel. It's lovely and light textured and gives skin a nice sheen.

Self-heating Scrub

H$_2$O+ Sea Results Thermal-Active Skin Polisher is an exfoliator with a difference. When you massage it into damp skin, it heats up, which not only feels lovely but also has the handy benefit of causing pores to expand and expel all their gunk. After one go of it, you will notice a difference, especially on the nose area – great if you happen to suffer from a blackheady nose as I do, bah.

Congestion Busting

Stand up, Origins Modern Friction. I have never, ever encountered a product that works as well and as consistently as this. It's creamy, soft-textured and an absolute wonder at smoothing flaky patches and getting rid of those pesky areas of congestion. Simply brilliant.

AISLING'S PICK

If you're looking for a scrub recommendation, Origins Modern Friction is it. Adored by gazillions for all the right reasons, this stuff is packed full of gorgeous botanic ingredients like rice starch, lemon oil and aloe and will leave your skin super soft and utterly pampered. Origins calls it 'nature's gentle dermabrasion', and while it's sloughing off dead skin it also magically refines pores. This one's a keeper.

Just don't let it get in your eyes, though – it will hurt and leave you staggering blindly round the bathroom until you can wash it out!

Harto

Love this – it leaves skin so smooth. Would use it on the neck and chest the odd time too. It's a divil if you get it in your eyes though – sting city!

Kirstie

Love love love LOVE this product. It is quite literally indispensable.

Bunny

I am a big fan of exfoliating and have found the Yonka peel and more recently a Savage Beauty exfoliant to strike the right balance between effectiveness and gentleness.

Gio

I used to use the Origins Never A Dull Moment exfoliator but recently discovered the Dermalogica Daily Microfoliant – use it every other day and it is lovely!

Stila Petals Infusions Retexturizing Scrub

This is a wonderful scrub that contains sweet orange oil, lemon oil and mint essence, so it smells delicious. It's the finely milled marble that makes it superfine and gentle enough to use every day. Some exfoliators can feel like they're scraping the face off you – not this one. It leaves a smooth matte finish and is worth a try if you're after a gentle scrub.

Dermalogica Daily Microfoliant

Superfine, supereffective exfoliator that's gentle enough to use on a regular basis. Perfect for young and combination skin.

TEDDY BOBBS DIY MOMENT

Come on now – I'm not Oirland's top financial advisor for nothing. I would put money on the fact that most of us have made a DIY exfoliator at some stage in the game. Well, I would put money on if it wasn't all tied up in Brendan Investments. Arra, this is ridiculously easy to make with just a couple of ingredients from the press. Use granulated sugar mixed with a little bit of oil and rub into your *phisog*. That's it! This works as effectively as most simple shop-bought face scrubs and is a hell of a lot cheaper.

PRODUCTS OF YORE: Buf-Puf

Remember how Adrian Mole cleaned the bath with his mother's Buf-Puf? That said it all, really. A sponge that scoured the life out of your skin, Buf-Puf is still with us. Like most Products of Yore, it's been repackaged and given a more up-to-date look. The range has increased and it looks set to stay. Oh well. My advice? Use it to clean your bath.

WHY YOU PROBABLY DON'T NEED TONER

In the 1940s, make-up was removed with heavy-duty cleansers like cold cream. Thick and greasy, these cleansers needed more than water to shift their residue and leave the pores unblocked, so toner was used to cut through the grease.

Often alcohol-based, toner can be harsh and disruptive to the skin. Modern cleansers have been formulated to rinse right off, ensuring skin is left clean and fresh with absolutely no requirement for a separate toner.

I don't believe toner is a necessary part of a skincare routine any more, but if you've got oily skin, you might like to use rosewater as a toner. Check the toner you use to make sure it's not loaded with alcohol – many of the most popular ones are. If you see the sales assistants cleaning the glass counters with the toner they're selling, that's a sure-fire red flag! I'm not making it up – this does happen.

Tina10

I don't user toner either, and I completely agree that it was for Days of Yore to cut through the grease left by cleansers. I think these days you are just stripping your skin of its own natural oils.

2

Dream Cream

Skin drinks up rich, nourishing creams and products with lovely essential oils.

Once you've got your cleanser down pat, it's time to turn your attention to the next step: moisturiser. This is another beauty step that can be a bit of a nightmare to perfect, hitting on the one for you may be a bit like the hunt for Mr Right. You'll probably kiss a lot of frogs, but when you get to the right Kermit, you'll know it's the one for you.

There are two types of moisturisers the majority of us splash the cash on – ones for day, and ones for night. But some people leave off the night cream, a step I'd always advise you to include. Skip to the end of the chapter to read my impassioned defence for the use of a special regime at night.

MOISTURISERS FOR DEHYDRATED SKIN

I've got skin that seems to dehydrate like Sub-Saharan Africa and it can be a constant battle to keep it moisturised. I'm ever mindful that even temporary wrinkles caused by dehydration will stay around forever if I don't get that skin moisturised. If this has happened to you, it's likely you've crossed the no-man's-land of 30-plus, when skin can seem to change overnight. You may suddenly find that the lovely light moisturiser you got on so well with in your 20s hates you and has cracked your face. But even if you don't have the same problem as me (yet, mwahaha), make sure you follow these steps.

1. Take off your make-up at night – every night!
2. Use a facial oil/serum/good night cream
3. Use a good day cream. If it doesn't have SPF included, then use a sunscreen on top.

4. Use a foundation that moisturises, reflects light and doesn't cling to lines.

5. Drink plenty of water.

Dehydrated skin drinks up rich, nourishing creams and products with lovely essential oils. These are what I turn to when the going gets tough.

DOES YOUR DAY MOISTURISER NEED TO HAVE SPF INCLUDED?

No, it doesn't. While it's handy not to have to apply another product, you'll often get better results if you put on your moisturiser, allow it to sink in and then put sunblock over the top. See Chapter 3 for tips on good facial sunblocks.

DAY CREAMS

Elizabeth Arden Intervene Pause & Effect Moisture Cream

A preventative cream for women in the 30–45 age group, this aims to halt the ageing process. Nice texture and smell, absorbs well and has an SPF of 15 – all the essentials. While it is pricey – oh, is it worth it.

~Thalia~
My holy grail moisturiser is Estée Lauder DayWear – the green one with SPF 15. It smells divine, like cucumbers – really fresh and it does the job for me!

xgirl

I'm using Elave's Daily Skin Defence SPF30 at the moment. I like the protection levels, though I find it a wee bit shiny. Not the same horrible shine I get from chemical sunscreens, though. I just use powder over it to take the shine down. Other than that it's a nice product – my skin is lovely and soft, with no dry patches and no congestion.

Dreamgirl

My best moisturiser is definitely Dermalogica's Active Moist. I find it's the only one that doesn't sting or take long to absorb … It'd be one of my desert island products!

Ro

I love my Lancôme Bienfait Multi-Vital Fluid. It's got protection against UVA and UVB with an SPF of 30.

Nivea Natural Beauty Radiance Boosting Moisturiser

This is a lovely, thick cream that's ideal for 20-somethings. The hint of shimmer in the formulation makes it ideal for wearing solo on good skin days.

Liz Earle Superskin Moisturiser

Let me count the ways I adore this product. It's got a gorgeous rich texture, contains tons of goodies like rosehip and cranberry oil and will soothe dry skin in a jiffy. It smells a bit odd, thanks to the fact that no fragrance was used in the formula, but once you see the results, you stop caring about that, let me tell you.

GREEN AND GORGEOUS: Dr. Hauschka Rose Day Cream

This is a loverly day moisturiser that is literally bursting with freshness and natural fragrance. 'Like applying a flower garden to your face every morning,' said a friend of mine who swears by it. Also available in a light version for those of you who found the original too rich.

BOTANICAL-PACKED FACIAL OILS

If there's a person still alive who doesn't know how much I love facial oils, then hopefully this will help to spread the word further. Put simply, these are the best thing for skin since … well, since anything, really. Dry skin will literally drink in facial oils and it's not an exaggeration to say you will notice instant results. Like, the next morning.

As a bonus, many of the facial oils around are pure botanicals, meaning they are the ultimate green and gorgeous pick. Trilogy, Burt's Bees, Kimia and Liz Earle all do sumptuous oils that I love.

Trilogy Certified Organic Rosehip Oil

From New Zealand comes the Trilogy brand. Try their Rosehip Oil, a gorgeous, silky oil that's really nourishing – rose in particular is great for dry and older skintypes.

Bobbi Brown EXTRA Face Oil

This is like a drink of water for skin that's incredibly dry. It sinks in really quickly and smells absolutely gorgeous too.

Tesco Bnatural Face Oil

Organic certification makes this supermarket facial oil stand out – and it's a great price.

Foxglove

I'm gonna rate very highly Decléor Hydra Floral Flower Nectar Moisturizing Cream. I use the jar and it's got this little tiny spatula with which you scoop some cream. I'd definitely recommend using this cos it prevents 'over-dosing' … this cream feels so pampering without being heavy, it feels cool on the skin, it sort of makes skin look radiant in a way, and if you like to feel your skin moist for hours, this is the one. Oh, and the smell is divine!

Em

Like Foxglove, I love Decléor's Hydra Floral. I've been using it along with the Decléor Aromessence Neroli and they work so well together. The moisturiser seems to sink in even quicker when I use the neroli and they both smell gorgeous too.

AISLING'S PICK:
Green and Gorgeous: Kimia

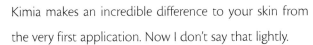

Kimia makes an incredible difference to your skin from the very first application. Now I don't say that lightly.

The Kimia Exquisite Rejuvenating Facial System is really simple to use despite its long-winded name. All it takes is a few squirts of the face oil and then the hydra activator.

If your skin is dry, this will help to put the moisture back in, plump up lines and give you a fresher, younger look.

Packed full of organic botanicals, this is a real treat. Apparently Victoria Beckham loves Kimia and I'm with Posh on this one. Taste in husbands? Check.* Love of Kimia? Double check. (*Though it's safe to say that Kimia won't cheat on you with Rebecca Loos, so that makes it even better.)

THE SKIN-DRYING EFFECT
OF RADIATORS

Bord Gáis rings up every year to say, 'Your boiler is due a service. Do you want to book in?'

'Sure,' I say, not really wanting to pay to get the feckin' boiler serviced but knowing that I have to.

When the Bord Gáis man rang me this year, we had a bit of a chat about the nip in the air and other related topics. 'I just put on the heating this morning for the first time this year,' sez I.

'I did myself too,' sez Bord Gáis man. 'Well you know, I wouldn't have bothered, but sure, I knew the wife would be down the stairs and she feels the cold. You know what women are like.'

'I do indeed,' I agreed.

But whenever the damn radiators go on, I notice my skin drying out. Even my hands get dry and crinkly.

I had a madly eccentric teacher in secondary school who used to bring a bowl of water into every class with her when the radiators were on. 'To put moisture back into the air, darlings,' she would tell us. 'Good for the skin.'

We used to snicker at the time, but you know, she was right. I'm putting bowls of water beside the radiators now too.

Malooba
My mum does this all the time; I find it does make a difference. Apparently it's also good if you have wooden furniture, as it prevents it drying out and cracking (a bit like skin really).

Ellenwaxer
You could also put a few drops of essential oil in the water and that'd replace any plug-in type scent things.

MAMMY SAYS

The way I look at it, it's only grease at the end of the day. Astral cream for me at night-time. 'Tis only fabilis. I've told all my girls about it and Aoife doesn't use anything else. Nuala now, she's a different story altogether – but sure, you can't be telling her anything. When is she giving me my day out? I've my lilac suit all picked out and everything.

Christine

My mother has used Astral for years and nothing else and she has the best skin – not one wrinkle at almost 60! It's worth a try!

Betty

I've pretty dry skin and a friend tipped me off to Astral, which is so cheap that most people would ignore it! But it's a rich cream which I find leaves my skin lovely and dewy in the morning. My friend's mother and grandmother use it too! Joanna Lumley is always raving about it, so that's good enough for me.

AISLING SAYS

Mammy's right. If you have something that works for you as a daily moisturiser, it doesn't matter a damn how much it costs. If you have robust skin that's not sensitive, you'll probably get on very well with the likes of Astral, Nivea and the supermarket brands. While the high-end brands are luxurious and smell lovely, if you're young or have great skin, you most likely don't need them. Once you're moisturising, that's the important thing. Do use your sunscreen over them though.

MOISTURISERS FOR OILY SKIN

Oily skin needs a light touch and a specially formulated moisturiser. Don't feel that because your skin is oily that it needs a good scrub with caustic soda and a Brillo pad every morning to dry it out and leave it at that. If you pick moisturisers that are targeted towards your skintype, they will work in conjunction with your other skincare. People with oily skin often avoid products with oil in them, but if you're buying good-quality skincare with natural essential oils in it, then there's no reason to shy away.

Best Products for Night

Vichy Normaderm Anti-Imperfection Hydrating Care

This promises to transforms skin in four weeks. If you use it in conjunction with a good cleanser for oily skin, it will really help with blemishes and too much oil being produced.

Yon-Ka Phyto 58

A salon brand that has impressive results with oily skin. Check this out if you're at the end of your tether.

Best Products for Night

Decléor Ylang Ylang Night Balm

There exists a philosophy in some skincare ranges that like should be treated with like. Decléor, Liz Earle and Dr. Hauschka all agree with this belief and as such will treat oily and spot-prone skin with oil. This waxy balm delivers a glow while helping to decongest skin.

Poppins
Yon-Ka Phyto 58 night cream is brill. Only started using it in the last six weeks. Has completely stopped all blemishes, always got them around no baby time but it has put an end to them! Anyways, everyone should use a night cream.

Tiptoe Shortbread

I have oily skin and the Decléor balm that I use is for oily skin specifically. I was pretty apprehensive at first cos it's a balm, but you only use a tiny bit and my skin is SO much better since I started using it!

Atomic_Blonde

Decléor is very good for oily skin, the ylang ylang Tippy uses is very good for oily skin. I use Essential Balm, which is more for normal/combo skin.

Trillion

I used the Lancôme Primordiale range before, and recently switched to cheaper brands because of the price. I've tried various No. 7, Boots and Nivea moisturisers with no success, and have worked out that I would have spent less money if I'd just bought the Lancôme one in the first place! (And not have six different unwanted moisturisers sitting on my dresser.)

Vichy Normaderm Nuit

It refines pores, mattifies oil-slick T-zones and calms down problem skin as you sleep. It's also really easy to get your paws on and it's a good price. What's not to like?

PRODUCTS OF YORE:
Clinique Computer

I'm calling this a Product of Yore because it flippin' well should be one. With all the diagnostic sophistication of an abacus, it is totally cringe-making if a sales assistant heaves this out from under the counter. At least it weathered the Y2K changeover well, so that was a plus for it anyway. However, at the time this book went to press, it was still in evidence at Clinique counters everywhere. It's been joined by the Clinique Diagnostic Mirror, so hopefully this will herald the farewell of the 'Computer'.

Moisturisers for Sensitive and Rosacea-prone Skin

Rosacea is extreme sensitivity of the skin. There are two types of rosacea, which can often coexist.

- Inflammatory – spots, angry outbreaks.
- Background – redness.

What Causes It?

Rosacea is largely genetic, but there are certain things that can make it worse. For example, certain foods (spicy) and drinks (red wine) can make rosacea-prone skin flare like a nuclear reactor. Get to know which foods make your skin react – and stay away from them.

Interestingly enough, rosacea has the highest incidence in Celtic skin. This is because we tend to have fair skin that's extremely photosensitive and can overreact to harsh environments, such as rain and wind, which we have in spades.

A good sun cream is absolutely essential for anyone with rosacea. Plaster on that factor 50 and you'll find there's a huge improvement. I recommend La Roche-Posay Anthelios SPF50+ because it's gentle and non-reactive. Try the tips and products over the page, they should help.

Cathyfly

I started using night creams regularly about a year ago (probably due to beaut.ie!) as I do think that especially as you get older your skin needs more help renewing itself during the night. I like Elizabeth Arden Good Night's Sleep too and am currently using Origins Night-A-Mins, which I picked up at the airport and am really liking it. It's sort of a cross between a cream and a serum and comes in a little glass medicine bottle. It's got aromatherapy-type thingies in it to help you sleep better too! I also use my Dermalogica Skin Smoothing Cream at night, as apparently it's suitable for use at night as well as during the day.

LanaLamont

Got a cheapy bottle (€9) of Dead Sea Spa Magik night moisturiser recently. Thrilled with it, really moisturising, my skin is lovely and soft, smooth in the morning and not greasy.

- Use a high-factor sun cream.
- Seavite is a wonderfully calm, soothing seaweed-based range. Natural and free from chemicals, your skin will sigh with relief when you apply it. I love the moisturising day cream. Available in chemists, health shops and Debenhams.
- Dermalogica Sheer Tint Redness Relief SPF 15 is slightly tinted and will both soothe and disguise redness. Brilliant stuff. I'd especially recommend this for guys, as they can't resort to make-up to cover things up. Well, of course they can if they want, but they might prefer to go this route! Available from salons and online.

If you're going through an inflammatory stage of rosacea, you will benefit from a course of IPL laser. Consult a dermatologist to get this done rather than a salon, plus check out Chapter 1 for recommendations for great ranges for sensitive skin.

Great Picks for Sensitive Skin

Your skintype is probably the one that's *not* suited to trying out action-packed night creams and serums, so my recommendation is to find a good product that provides excellent emollient properties and stick with it.

Seavite Organic Seaweed Face Creme

Find this in chemists and be amazed at how great your skin will look. Specifically developed for those with sensitive skins, in particular I'm loving the face creme, which you can use as both a day and night product. Trust me, it leaves your skin *so* soft. Developed here in Ireland with love and care, this is a natural, seaweed-based collection of creams, masks, shower, bath, hair and body products.

Clinque Redness Solutions Daily Protective Base SPF 15

Apply this after your moisturiser for a double-whammy of redness protection. A green tint takes down redness and chemical-free sunscreens protect your delicate complexion from the sun's rays.

La Roche-Posay Toleriane Soothing Protective Care

Extremely kind and gentle to sensitive skin and skin that is prone to flare up at the slightest touch, this is also well priced and available nationwide.

Aveeno Ultra-Calming Moisturizing Cream

Cheap as the proverbial chips and completely brilliant as a moisturiser for any skintype. Dry skins love it, but it was actually formulated specially for sensitive types. Packed full of feverfew, it smells great too.

Krista
I use Lancôme Neurocalm Night Cream and absolutely love it. I am 25 and get a bit of rosacea. Using this really calms my skin.

MASKS

There are masks out there for all manner of issues and needs and they can be a brilliant add-on to your skincare routine.

GREAT FOR HUNGOVER SKIN

Dermalogica Multivitamin Power Recovery Masque is known on Beaut.ie as the 'orange burn victim mask' because this is what you'll look like with it on, gooey and dripping with orange slime. But it's nourishing and super hydrating and it infuses your skin with vitamins – essential for hangover recovery. As with all face masks, just hope no one calls to the door.

Fletch
Going to do my Dermalogica Multivitamin tonight, it really is a miracle worker! Makes your skin feel so soft and de-stressed!

Dellie
Dermalogica Multivit is brill and the best beauty investment that I've made!

Great for Dry Skin

Great at de-crocodiling skin is Estée Lauder's Hydra Complete Multi-Level Moisture Gel Mask. It's really hydrating and great after a day spent in biting winds, drying air-con or just any time you feel your face needs a bit of a treat.

Great for Oily Skin

Head straight to your nearest Prescriptives stockist and grab a tube of their Instant Gratification Skin Renewal Peel. A double-duty product, it's an exfoliator and mask built into one. Whack this self-heating stuff onto skin, let it do its job and wash off. *Voilà* – a fresh, shiny-bright face, with congestion seriously addressed.

Great for Sensitive Skin

Delivering a difference in minutes, RoC's Calmance Soothing Regenerating 5 Minute Mask is great. Presented in six nifty monodoses to keep the product fresh, it leaves you with calmer, less irritated cheeks. Impressed? Oh, you betcha.

Aoife

I've just started using the Yes To Carrots mud mask, and it is amazing! I have quite good skin though, thank god, but during the winter there's two spots which go really dry and flaky. This is keeping my skin all smooth and lovely! (Also using their day cream and loving it.)

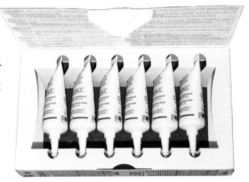

Great for Young Skin

The Body Shop's Blue Corn 3-in-1 Deep Cleansing Scrub Mask is terrific for normal to oily skin. Clay draws out impurities and blue corn buffs off gunk.

NIGHT FEVER

I was having a conversation with a friend last night and the talk turned (as it usually does) to all things beaut.ieful.

'But what do you really think of night creams?' she said. 'Is there really a difference between the night and day versions of a cream? Or is it all just a bit of a con to make you spend more money? And what about the Dr. Hauschka theory?' Gosh so many questions. Here are my answers.

- I love night creams. Probably because my skin can get pretty dry, I love nothing better than going to bed with a super-duper night cream on. I can almost feel it sinking in, working its creamy magic on any line that might be thinking of showing itself.

- While we sleep, cellular regeneration occurs and our skin renews itself. Night creams are specially formulated to help this process of renewal and are packed full of ingredients to repair and regenerate.

Paula
The rhythmic conditioners are designed to clear your skin of previous cosmetics, and it's natural for your skin to dry or even break out as those chemicals come out. Once your skin begins to produce its own oils again, you'll notice the benefits.

- Day cream is busy doing other stuff, shielding us from the environment, hydrating and protecting skin from the sun if it's got an SPF. Night cream uses the slumber-filled hours of darkness to work its magic, ensuring that you wake up with skin firmer and plumper than normal.

- Something to consider is Dr. Hauschka's theory that we shouldn't use night cream, but that doesn't suit everyone.

If you've got young skin, don't worry too much about the brand of your night cream – use the night cream from the brand that you use during the day. You won't need the expensive, science-packed creams yet.

Dr. Hauschka Rhythmic Night Conditioner

If you've got dry and sensitive skin, it can be positively shocking to be told that there is a whole range of skin care that recommends no night cream while you sleep.

The Dr. Hauschka range is holistic, all natural and cruelty free. Your mood, the seasons and the way your body works are all taken into account to ensure you are getting optimum benefit from your skincare.

It's a very different way to treat your skin, though – a way that can seem strange to those of us used to traditional skincare regimes. There are seven steps to perfect skin the Dr. Hauschka way, and one of the most important of these is: don't use night cream.

Why on earth not? Dr. H reckons that while you sleep, your skin is naturally rebalancing itself and putting on night cream interferes with this natural process. Despite sounding like a skincare regime favoured by the Catholic Church, Rhythmic Night Conditioner contains water, essential oils and plant extracts and claims to bring skin to its natural balance in 28 days.

If you're brave enough to ditch the night cream for a month and can't find anything to suit your skin, it might just be worth giving this a try.

Glitterkitty

I'm still loving the Burt's Bees Carrot Night Creme ... for my dry, old smoker's skin it's fab. I'll be buying the Dermalogica Barrier Repair, which again I use under night cream a couple of times a week. This has definitely made a difference to the tiny red veins and general appearance of my skin.

Fifisparkle

I use the Estée Lauder Advanced Night Repair serum and find it great. Got a sample a while ago and LOVED the way it made my skin feel, so I splashed out at Christmas and bought myself a bottle! Have to keep it on a high shelf in the bathroom away from my toddler's reach or it would go straight down the toilet!

3

Erase and Rewind

...THERE ARE LOTS OF THINGS YOU CAN DO TO IMPROVE YOUR SKIN AND
KEEP IT LOOKING YOUNGER.

Tír na nÓg

In the land of Tír na nÓg, no one grows old or dies. Wanting for nothing, everyone stays young and healthy and beautiful, no one gets sick, wrinkly or turns grey. Sounds great, doesn't it? The downside is that you can never come home again – but sure, why would you care? You'd be out with the beautiful people every night, drinking mead and looking in mirrors.

Yes, it does sound a bit like Hollywood.

Niamh of the Golden Hair took a fancy to Oisin and spirited him off to the Irish version of Elysium on her magic horse (it's located out beyond Sligo somewhere). Oisin got homesick and wanted to return, not knowing that hundreds of years had passed in real time since his departure. Cutting straight to the chase, Niamh told him not to get off the horse or face dire consequences. Oisin, of course, got off the horse, instantly withered up and turned to dust.

Is it any wonder we're programmed to believe in anti-ageing miracles after being brought up with a legend like that?

We live in a culture obsessed with youth, and as we can see from legend, this preoccupation has existed for a long, long time. So of course lots of treatments and potions have been developed to try to retain that elusive youth. Bearing that in mind, there are lots of things you can do to improve your skin and keep it looking younger. Let's have a look.

CAUSES OF AGEING

There are two main causes of ageing. One is genetic, and in fairness there's not a lot we can do about that. The other is environmental and this is the one we can try to prevent. Sun damage is a huge cause of premature ageing. So are pollution, smoking, excessive alcohol and bad diet. Oh dear.

BY THE HOKEY

Why do men age so much better than women? It's all down to hormones. Men have much thicker and oilier skin than women and this means that they get wrinkly about 10 years later than us. Ten years! How unfair. But console yourself with the fact that when they do eventually get wrinkles, they'll be much deeper and more pronounced than ours.

DO ANTI-AGEING CREAMS REALLY WORK?

We all know a woman who never used anything on her face but Pond's Cold Cream and still looks fresh as a daisy at seventy. But that doesn't mean you are that woman, and the key with all anti-ageing products is to start young. Prevention is always better than cure, and here's a fact: if you have deep lines and wrinkles plus tons of sun damage, no cream will be able to give you back your teenage skin. Botox, fillers and surgery are the only things to sort you out in that case.

That's not to say that creams are ineffective — many contain lovely, moisture-rich, antioxidant-packed goodies that will only do your skin good. And don't forget, skincare science is constantly improving, as Boots proved with their year-long trial for Protect & Perfect Intense Beauty Serum.

Pseudoscience and Marketing

There's no doubt about it: beauty brands definitely prey on our darkest fears with their claims and advertising campaigns. So how do you get past the jargon on the box and work out if a product performs? Brands like Vichy and Lancôme – both part of the huge L'Oréal group – are good examples of companies that conduct in-depth scientific trials on new ingredients and products. Over time, what's learned in these trials trickles down to the cheaper brands like L'Oréal Paris, ensuring that you get good results at good prices.

Strength of Ten Tigers

Just to throw something else into the mix: if an ingredient or product does work – and some, like Retinol (also known as vitamin A) definitely do, the strongest dosage is often only available at the dermatologist's office. Many pharmacy lines like RoC's Retin-Ox, Vichy's LiftActiv Retinol HA Total Wrinkle Care and Boots Protect & Perfect range contain varying strengths of vitamin A derivatives, but the top-dollar – and most effective – version can only be got on prescription.

CHEAP CREAMS = VERY SMALL AMOUNTS OF ACTIVE INGREDIENTS

Most anti-ageing products contain beneficial ingredients – but only in tiny amounts because they're expensive, and such tiny amounts won't do any good. This means that cheap creams can make misleading anti-ageing claims. Sad to say, but the more expensive the product, the more likely it is to contain higher concentrations of the good stuff.

THE BRANDS TO BUY

You can drop serious cash on products and be disappointed when they don't perform, and what works for one person may not work for you – everyone's skin is different and has different issues. But I recommend Estée Lauder for research-led, department store skincare, RoC, Boots and Vichy for excellence in the pharmacy sector (they're both French, and we know how well Gallic women look, eh?) and L'Oréal Paris and Olay for supermarket ranges that provide good anti-ageing benefits.

Then there's the whole 'Doctor' area of 'cosmeceutical' products. A mix of cosmetic and pharmaceutical, the term is applied to products that are almost medical-grade and which contain lots of active ingredients and heavy-duty anti-ageing capabilities. I highly rate the Murad range, created by Dr Howard Murad. He's the man behind research into AHAs, he's pushed and pioneered research into antioxidants and pomegranate technology, and he's an all-round whizz at the business of skin.

JOWLS

Jowls are one of the biggest indicators of age, and whether you'll get them or not is largely genetic. There are science-packed explanations for this, of course, but one sentence sums up the whole process. As we age, the fat in our faces 'falls' from our cheeks down to our jaw. Yes, really.

Unfortunately, there's not a lot that can naturally be done about this. Injectibles like Sculptra will fatten up cheeks, but to target the jowls, you'll need something more drastic. Good creams and facial massage can play a part in improving things, but to reverse the jowling action you'd need to consider a surgical treatment. However, if that's a step too far, you can think about my next tip instead.

Jowl No More with a Good Haircut

A good hairstyle works wonders to take attention from jowls, as it does for many of the signs of ageing. Worried about a wrinkly forehead? Cut a fringe, as I heard a hairdresser cheerfully advise a client who had this concern. This same hairdresser advises a flattering layered style above shoulder level if you're worried that you look more bulldog than chiselled lovely, and it's a hell of a lot cheaper than anything more drastic.

TROUT POUT

From Mickey Rooney to Leslie Ash, the celebrity world is full of lip plump horrors. The lips are one of the parts of the face to show age by getting thinner and losing volume, thus inciting the current craze for injections into the lips to make them look fuller. But if you've no intention of going for a full-on lip plumping injectible, what about those lip plumpers like Too Faced Lip Injection – do they work, I hear you ask? Well, no, not really. What they do is irritate the skin, causing it to swell slightly and temporarily. It's an unpleasant sensation and it doesn't last. See Chapter 14 for tricks to make your lips look a little fuller with make-up.

Botox

Ah, good old Botox. No one will ever admit to getting it done, no matter how blatantly obvious it is. I've seen people who should know better tell porkies about it even when they can't raise their eyebrows any more. It works by freezing tiny muscles under the skin and evens out expression lines. Less is more with Botox, and the effects only last between two and four months, so even if you don't like the effect, you're not stuck with it. If you hate your crows' feet that much, give it a go. Remember, you don't have to tell anyone if you don't want to!

Also, remember that it doesn't matter how many names the cosmetic companies make up that kind of sound like Botox, like Boswellox and so on – they're not Botox. If you want the real thing, you have to get the injections. Don't get it done by a beautician or a nurse in any type of salon, though – they're not properly trained no matter what they say. Go to a doctor or a dermatologist who has qualifications and knows what they're doing. And if you even think of going to a Botox party, you'll have me to deal with.

Like death and taxes, Botox is one thing in life you can be sure of. It works.

WORK OF SATAN: Cigarettes

If you want to age at warp speed, dry out your skin and give a convincing impression of a heavily lined leather handbag, then by all means, smoke. Added benefits include stinking like an ashtray, all your clothes stinking, attractive deep lines around your lips, looking older than your non-smoking mates and setting yourself up for lung cancer and other diseases. So sure, it's a free country – you decide when you're outside in the cold and rain on a fag break.

CELEBRITY BEAUTY SECRETS: Debbie Harry

Debbie Harry uses lamb embryos to keep herself looking young. And not any old lamb embryos – they must be black lambs. Why? No idea, but that's the crazy old world of celeb beauty secrets, eh? She's been having these 'fresh cell' injections since she was 35 and proclaims them to be a logical response to the ageing process – simply getting new cells injected into her face.

Well, we can all see how well that approach is working. So if you're joining a queue to get this done, I ask – do you need your head examined? Baa to that.

SUN DAMAGE

A couple of years ago, I went for a skin analysis to see how much sun damage I had on my face. Although I did go on sun holidays when I was young, I didn't go on loads. (I had plenty of sunny summers in Tramore, though.) I never wore any suncream on my face. I didn't know you had to. If you didn't come home with a tan, sure, you might as well not have bothered going away, was the popular assumption. Fake face tan was unheard of.

Even so, I was unprepared for the results. The skin on my face was showing sun damage to the tune of 23 per cent. Nearly a quarter of the skin on my face is irreparably damaged – and this is well above average.

So what can I do? Well, nothing is the answer. All I can do is try to prevent any more damage occurring by using high-factor sunblock on my face.

Now that we know that the sun is the leading cause of preventable ageing, there's no reason why everyone shouldn't be slathering on the sun protection.

Top Tip: Put your sun cream on after your moisturiser and get as high a factor as possible to protect your skin.

Ghost Face

Many high-protection face creams can leave you with a deathly white pallor. Obviously not the carefree summer look you were intending to convey.

Why the heck does this happen? It's down to the use of physical sunblockers like zinc, often used in the ingredients mix. Zinc can make the cream stay looking white – even if you've been frantically rubbing it in for ages. And while this may be tolerable on the rest of your body, it sure ain't going to pass muster on the visage. Lots of creams have been formulated to take this into consideration – here are a few I like.

La Roche-Posay Anthelios SPF 50+

This is a brilliant sun protection product for the face. Absolutely perfect for everyday use, it won't irritate and works well with foundation. It doesn't leave that nasty white ghost face and it's available in most chemists. There's also a tinted version, which means you can ditch the foundation altogether if you prefer.

Hamilton Everyday Face SPF 30+

The Hamilton range originates in Australia, where they know a thing or twenty about sun protection. It's inexpensive and it works well.

Vichy Capital Soleil SPF 50+

A brilliant product, available in every chemist at a great price. I always have a tube of this on the go.

Chanel UV Essentiel Protective UV Care Anti-Pollution SPF50+

If you're feeling flush, then you might want to splash out on this fantastic sunscreen from Chanel. It smells only gorgeous and like the others, there's no ghost face. It's good for oilier skins due to a mattifying effect and provides a great base for make-up for any skin type.

Gracie
I really like Clinique City Block. I have a gold-tinted version too, which makes me all glowy as well as protected.

Tina10
I have the Dermalogica Solar Defence, the little bottle that you mix in with your moisturiser or foundation to give you factor 30 protection. I really like it – it works and doesn't make me break out.

15 + 15 DOES NOT EQUAL 30. IT EQUALS 15.

The laws of mathematics are turned on their head here. You can't add the SPF of your moisturiser to the SPF of your foundation to make a new super breed of sun protection. So if you use a moisturiser with SPF 25 and apply a foundation with an SPF 15 over it, this will not create SPF 40. It just means you have SPF 25 – the highest of the products.

Top Tip: Your foundation will also add a measure of protection, as the pigment acts as a physical blocker to the sun's ray.

BALLS TO THAT

I'm sure every one of us has experienced this problem at some stage: you've bought a new super-duper anti-ageing cream with SPF to find to your dismay that it's not sinking in and is all rolling off your face in little lumps. The high level of active ingredients contained in good anti-ageing creams can react with SPF, causing moisturiser to ball up on the skin.

This can also happen if silicone is present in the product. And it might not happen to everyone – it can depend on your skin type.

If it happens, there's nothing to do but throw the moisturiser into the bin in disgust – or give it to someone else. What a feckin' waste of money.

Freeze 24-7 Instant Gratification

This is expensive stuff for sure, but if you want something to temporarily (very temporarily – think 24 hours) make your lines disappear, then this will do the trick. Apply a little bit of this directly onto any fine lines and you should see a noticeable reduction in appearance. Like Arnold Schwarzenegger, they'll be back, but you'll get your quick fix. The lines must be fine, though – this won't work if you've got grooves you could park a bike in.

SERUM

A good serum is a wonder and a joy. Now before you say to yourself, 'Pah – this is just another "thing" to buy', let me make the case for serum. Serums really work. I can honestly vouch for them – supercharged with concentrated doses of vitamins, packed with intensive skin-nourishing ingredients, I think they're a must for serious skincare devotees. Applying a couple of squirts of serum before moisturiser is the best thing you can do for your skin.

Kirstie

Try using Origins A Perfect World White Tea Skin at night to help fight free radicals that have built up during the day. It's gorgeous and nourishing too. The thing with serum is you use very little – 1–2 drops is all you need. You only need one drop of L'Oréal's concentrated Derma Genesis serum.

Babaduck

I've been using the Boots P&P serum for a year and really like it – as I don't smoke, I've fewer lines than others the same age.

Great Serums Picks

The ones I've tried – and would buy again.

Vichy Aqualia

Designed as a hydrating add-on for any skincare regime, regardless of skin type, Vichy's Aqualia range contains a fantastic, inexpensive serum. You'll get it at the chemist, and it's a great first step if you're twenty-something and would like to add a little more to your daily routine. But if you're sixty and would like a boost too, then it's equally as good.

No7 Protect & Perfect Intense Beauty Serum

God, remember the brouhaha when Professor Regan made her discovery that Boots Perfect & Protect actually worked? Mass hysteria ensued (in the UK anyway) and the Boots marketing machine went into overdrive, quickly capitalising on the success of this product with complementary lotions and potions. Now they've launched Protect & Perfect Intense Beauty Serum, designed for deeper lines and wrinkles – and they've proven it works.

Estée Lauder Advanced Night Repair

Estée Lauder Advanced Night Repair is loved by millions. It's an oldie, but boy, is it a goodie. Slightly evil-smelling, I adore it – and as the name says, this one is for night-time use only.

Prescriptives Super Line Preventer Xtreme

Light and quickly absorbed, Prescriptives Super Line Preventor Xtreme reminds me of the Estée Lauder product on the left, as it's another orange gloop that does your skin *so* much good. A bit expensive, but worth it.

Lancôme Genetique

They say it acts as an insurance policy – for your skin and that it's suitable for all ages. We reckon it softens skin and helps to keep lines and wrinkles in check.

Also Recommended: L'Oréal DermaGenesis Serum.

HAVE A LITTLE PATIENCE

In the immortal words of Gary Barlow, I exhort you to have a little patience. It takes any new skincare regime six weeks to three months to establish itself. If you see an immediate improvement, this is because the product is increasing hydration and temporarily plumping up the skin. Any longer-lasting results will take a bit of time. Remember this before you give up any new lotions and potions because they 'don't work'.

Tigerlily
Burt's Bees Rosehip Serum is nice for around the eyes at night.

Tina
Dermalogica Skin Hydrating Booster is just amazing if your skin needs hydrating.

Lou Lou
I use Botanics Radiance Night Renewal Serum under my night cream and in the morning my skin is lovely and soft.

Miss_M
I have been using serums under my moisturiser for the last 14 or 15 years. I live in a large city with tons of pollution and I believe the serum works as a barrier between my skin and all the gunk that flies around in the air. I've used EL Advanced Night Repair for years, which I really like, but at the moment I use L'Oréal Derma Genesis serum or Olay Regenerist serum.

Cleanser

You'll find that as your skin gets older, you'll want to turn to more gentle forms of cleansing. Anything foaming, soap based or in any way harsh should be avoided. Take your make-up off with a good cream or milk cleanser. Also, be gentle with your skin. After forty, it gets considerably thinner and you don't want to be scrubbing away with any type of harsh cleanser.

The easiest way to choose a cleanser is to pick the complementary product to your moisturiser. So if you're a RoC gal, you might like to use the RoC cleanser, but if you'd like to try something new, here are some recommendations.

Great Cleansers for Anti-ageing
Shu Uemura Cleansing Beauty Oil Premium

I'm a bit evangelical about oil cleansers, as you might have guessed by now. Shu Uemura's Cleansing Beauty Oil Premium is an anti-ageing, antioxidant-packed product that removes even the most stubborn of slap. This stuff emulsifies with water into a milk, which washes the day off really well. Kéraskin also do a nice version, called Huile Nudité, an ideal substitute if you can't lay your paws on the Shu version.

Murad Essential-C Cleanser

Gel cleansers are ideal for use in the shower because you need water to make them work and they're oh so quick and easy. Use a gel cleanser in the morning before moisturising and make-up.

I rate Murad's Essential-C Cleanser. It's vitamin packed and excellent for anti-ageing, as it helps to purify environmentally damaged skin.

Eve Lom Cleanser

There's a reason this stuff ends up on 'best of' lists all the time, and that's because, to paraphrase Tina Turner, it's simply the bee's knees. It's Eve Lom's amazing cleanser, and it's a gorgeous product that makes skin clean and soft in one, plus it plumps out fine lines as it's so moisturising – so you look younger. Aromatherapy oil packed, you use it with a muslin cloth to gently exfoliate skin – and make-up doesn't stand a chance against it.

Also Recommended: Origins A Perfect World Deep Cleanser with White Tea.

DAY CREAMS

Moisture and sun protection are your two big areas of concern. Look for creams as opposed to fluids, as ageing skin needs products that are rich in things like essential fatty acids and ceramides. These soothe skin, protect its barrier function and provide heavy-duty hydration. Oils are also a brilliant choice for ageing skin, as they gently slough off dead skin cells, helping to reveal a brighter complexion. Here are a few good hydrating day moisturisers.

Dr Nick Lowe Super Charged SPF15 Day Cream

This is a surprisingly affordable and high-quality range of skincare. Unlike other 'Doctor' brands, which may be great but are usually expensive, this is affordable. With all sorts of sciencey ingredients and SPF, this is a great product.

Murad Perfecting Day Cream SPF 30

Super-duper moisturising and in possession of an excellent SPF of 30, mature and dry skin types will drink this thick, comforting moisturiser up.

Clinique Superdefense SPF 25

Nice consistency and it does the all-important sinking in quickly and efficiently, providing a great base for make-up. Plus, it's packed full of anti-ageing ingredients, antioxidants and SPFs. All good stuff.

PinkPanther

I love Superdefense – though I can't say it's really helped with my emotional stress. It's a lovely base for make-up and doesn't leave skin greasy.

But apparently, it is also *armed to fight emotional stress*. You wha?

That makes it sound like it will sit in traffic for you, deal with your most difficult clients in work, have a quick argument with himself when you come home and pick the kids up from the crèche, and possibly deal with a house move and a messy divorce.

But seriously now. The emotional thing is to do with inflammation. Clinique's theory is that constant, chronic stress leads to a low-level inflammation in the cells, causing them to degrade and die quicker. This moisturiser apparently deals with this problem.

Guinot Age Nutritive

The pot is shaped like a little spaceship, which is almost enough to get it into my top day creams list all on its own, but this is a beautiful product though it is hideously expensive. With a thick, slightly gel-like texture, it smoothes on well, provides excellent hydration and a good base for make-up. Oh, and it smells great, too.

Darphin Fibrogène Cream

My skin adores this. And sure, it'd want to, considering the extortionate price, wha? This is a thick, white balm that you really have to work out of the pot. A little goes a long way and it's a skin saviour for really dry skin that's stressed and showing a lot of dehydration lines.

Garnier Vital Restore

Flower Power ladies will love the flower power of this hydrating and firming cream. Aimed at the over-50s, it addresses pigmentation too.

Also Recommended: Shiseido Benefiance, NutriPerfect Day Cream SPF 15, Olay Total Effects Day.

IN THE NIGHT GARDEN

Night cream is really where it's all at when it comes to fabulous anti-ageing products. As explained in Chapter 2, the hours of sleep are the time that the body uses to renew and regenerate itself. Supporting this process with a good anti-ageing night cream will work wonders for your skin, and if you're going to spend, this is the area to do it in.

Let's have a look at purse-friendly creams – and sure, while we're at it, we might as well see some really expensive ones too.

Shopping Trolley Best Buys

There's no doubt about it – it is just so easy to buy skincare in the supermarket and there are some fantastic ranges on the shelves. But there are also a lot of crap ones, so when you're dashing through the aisles with two screaming kids hanging off the side of the trolley, it helps to know what's good so you can grab it and go.

Just economise elsewhere by buying own-brand groceries. They taste the same – well, not really, but being beautiful will be worth it. Don't tell the other half what you're up to though – he won't understand.

Olay Total Effects Night Firming Cream

The Olay stable of skin creams is famous for being the affordable face of anti-ageing skincare. You honestly can't go wrong with Olay – throw the Night Firming Cream into yer basket. To take things up a notch, you could also try the Regenerist range for even more science.

L'Oréal Paris Derma Genesis Serum Concentrate

Love them or hate them, L'Oréal is one of the biggest cosmetic companies in the world. From Maybelline, Lancôme and Vichy to The Body Shop and Kérastase, they're all owned by L'Oréal. This means that while all these companies operate independently to develop products and bring them to market, there is also an element of knowledge sharing. L'Oréal Paris skincare is getting better and Derma Genesis with Pro-Xylane is another one to pop into the trolley. My pick is the fab serum.

Garnier UltraLift Pro-X

This is no-fuss skincare with an improved anti-ageing range. If you've got sensitive skin, skip this one.

Tesco Skin Wisdom Age Delay Night Cream

You'll only be cutting off your nose to spite your face if you turn it up at the Tesco Skin Wisdom range. Developed by holistic expert Bharti Vyas, it's cheap and it works – really well. Age Delay Night Cream is the one to go for here.

Mid-price Active Pick
RoC Retin-Ox Plus Night Cream

Dermatologists rate RoC's Retin-Ox line as the best thing before prescription Retin-A – and that's saying something. Retin-Ox Plus Night Cream contains ingredients that can help to repair and restore skin, and using it while you snooze is a fab way to see benefits. Great stuff.

Money to Burn

You can really let rip with anti-ageing night creams. From Crème de la Mer to Eve Lom, this is really a case of Money No Object. But seeing as money is a very important object for most of us, this is what I recommend.

First Signs of Ageing: Molton Brown Facezone Overnight Renewal

If you're starting to feel slightly crinkled, Facezone Overnight Renewal is a great first step into the world of luxury night creams. It smells of roses, is light and easily absorbed and glides on smoothly over a freshly cleansed face. In the morning, you'll wake with soft, glowing skin.

AISLING'S PICK: Gatineau Defi Lift 3D

This is the one I choose to snuggle up with every night. It's rare for me to repeat buy with skincare – there's always so many new things to try – but on my third jar of this, I realised I'd developed a relationship. Nothing else gives my dehydrated skin that firming moisture surge overnight.

Only Fabilis: Liz Earle Superskin Concentrate

Liz Earle Superskin Concentrate is an amazingly concentrated, fabulously scented night-time treat that will perk your skin up and leave you looking years younger the next day. Warm a couple of drops in your hands and massage into your face before snuggling down. This oil is one of the best around and I absolutely love it. You will too.

Prevage Anti-Aging Night Cream

Mad expensive, but I rate Elizabeth Arden and Allergan's Prevage Anti-Aging Night Cream. It's very fancy: the product is sealed within a posh jar that you have to press down to dispense, so the active ingredients stay potent for longer. On thirty-something skin it delivers smooth, even tone and hydration, and if you're older, you'll reap even more benefits.

Swit-Swoo Night Oil

If you're finding nothing's working for you, switch to an oil. Darphin's 8 Flower Nectar is a gem. All you need is one or two drops for your whole face, but it's so goodness-packed that that's enough. Use this for a week and be amazed at your lovely soft skin.

EYE CREAM

The skin around the eyes is so fine and thin that it starts to show signs of ageing way before the rest of your face. Plus this area has a tendency to dehydrate quickly, leaving you with horrible lines that are caused by lack of moisture. And that's moisture a cream can put back. You only need to use tiny amounts of eye cream, so you can splash out a bit here – the cream will last for absolutely ages. I actually can't remember how long my StriVectin lasts because my original purchase of it has been shrouded in the mists of time.

AISLING'S PICK: StriVectin-SD

This is a wonder cream for sure and if you're interested in staving off the appearance of those lines for as long as possible, you should invest in a tube. StriVectin was originally formulated for stretch marks, but it was quickly discovered that it was playing a blinder on wrinkles too. The original formulation included aromatherapy extracts that were causing irritation to eyes. StriVectin took the oils out of the mix and a star was born. Although there's a hefty price tag on this eye cream, a little goes a very long way indeed and it lasts for a very long time.

Elizabeth Arden Ceramide Gold Ultra Restorative Capsules

Oh so lovely! Little individual capsules for one treatment only. Break one open and spread it on the skin around your eyes at night-time. Nourishing and effective.

Vichy Aqualia Thermal Eyes

Satisfyingly cool to the touch and on the skin, this is de-puffing and fortifying and is ideal for under-eye bags and dark circles. Containing fancy-pants ingredients to hydrate the eye contour area, promote circulation and reduce swelling, bags are diminished and dark circles are reduced. Sing hosannas!

Clinique All About Eyes Rich

A firm favourite with twenty- and early thirty-somethings who don't need anything heavy duty, this keeps eyes fresh and hydrated.

Top Tip: You only need a dab of cream the size of a grain of rice for each eye. Any more and you risk overloading delicate skin, causing puffiness.

IN THE SALON: DO ANTI-AGEING FACIALS REALLY WORK?

Temporarily, yes. They can give you a fantastic lift and make everything appear tighter and firmer. You can prolong the effect by using good creams and following the therapists' recommendations – but sadly, as yet there's no such thing as a non-surgical facelift, despite what anyone says.

Looking after your skin with regular facials and getting into a good routine is always going to keep your skin younger looking, however, so book in for that course of treatments you've been promising yourself. They'll make you feel fantastic.

Five Anti-Ageing Salon Facials to Try

Reading a spa or salon treatment menu can be a bit like perusing the menu in a posh restaurant: confusing, not to mention expensive. But a bit of reading between the lines will help you to choose the treatment that's right for you. Look for words like 'oxygen', 'collagen', 'anti-oxidant', 'plumping' and 'renewing' and you'll be on the right track. And if in any doubt, ask your therapist – that's what she's there for.

Elemis

This lovely spa brand does several facials that provide good anti-ageing benefits. Pro-Collagen Quartz Lift Facial is a gentle treatment that's skin plumping, relaxing and comforting. The Tri-

Enzyme Resurfacing Facial is more suited for those with serious skin issues like deep lines and wrinkles, as it uses fruit enzymes to slough off the top layer of skin.

Guinot

It's a bit like being Frankenstein's monster: Guinot's Hydradermie facials use the Hydraderm machine, which you're attached to and grounded to the bed. Yikes! It's not as scary as it sounds, though, and there is a good reason: attached to the machine is a special wand which is used on skin for massage and lymphatic drainage. The facials are relaxing too, and the results speak for themselves: skin is fresher, brighter and plumper following a treatment.

Murad

For skin in need of a pit stop and for those suffering from sun damage and pigmentation, check out the Murad Environmental Shield Vitamin-C Infusion Facial. Packed full of skin-kindly vitamins, this treatment is antioxidant rich and helps to restore elasticity and firmness while fading pigmentation and smoothing out fine lines and wrinkles. Brilliant after a sun holiday, too.

Decléor

The Decléor Aroma Expert Hydraforce Facial begins with a relaxing back massage – ah, bliss – and infuses your skin with vitamin C, wild pansy, mint and orange floral waters. This facial is luxurious. It's indulgent. It's relaxing. And skin feels so nourished and hydrated afterwards. It's fantastic as a pick-me-up – it plumps up fine lines and if you're worried that the years might be taking their toll, then this is the facial for you. Highly recommended.

Gatineau

This luxurious range includes a couple of great anti-agers: the Hydro-Source Anti-Aging Facial is a replenishing, wrinkle-reducing treatment that's packed full of collagen. Expect lovely, plump, nourished skin with diminished fine lines and wrinkles. Oxygen is always a good bet and the Gatineau Oxygenating Relaxing Facial pushes H_2O into the skin, helping with cell renewal.

Microdermabrasion

Microdermabrasion is an incredibly effective form of exfoliation. This is a salon treatment using a wand full of ultrafine crystals that is passed over your face to scour away dead skin cells. The top (dead) layer of your skin is lifted away and skin looks more toned and refined, with the added bonus of fine lines appearing reduced. You'll find that your moisturiser sinks in better afterwards too.

I have to admit that I'm a fan of super-soft luxury facials, so I do feel like I'm being scoured by a Brillo pad during microdermabrasion. But to be honest, most people dismiss that as me being a bit of a wuss and I have friends who go for regular treatments. It doesn't hurt, it's just a bit uncomfortable. Afterwards, a soothing, moisturising mask will be plastered on and that makes me feel a bit more pampered.

There's no 'downtime' for microdermabrasion. No downtime = no redness or peeling, so there's no need to hide yourself away from the world. In fact, you can go straight off to work or the shops afterwards. Yeah, shopping sounds a lot better, doesn't it?

Home Microdermabrasion

If you don't feel like shelling out for a salon microdermabrasion, you could think of trying one of the 'at home' kits. While you won't get the same level of skin-scrubbing as you would in a salon, these products can be very effective, and usually take the form of a course of exfoliation and rich creams spread over a couple of weeks. You'll see the best results from these kits with younger skin (under the age of 35, say).

Lancôme Resurface Peel

For a home treatment, the Lancôme Resurface Peel kit is a very good buy. I often find that these home versions of salon treatments are quite frankly crap. They have to water them down (literally) so much that they can't possibly work.

Boredoffice girl

I've got very dry skin that's sensitive and I've had three sessions of microdermabrasion. Your skin is pinkish for maybe two days and feels sandblasted, so put on plenty of moisturiser/aloe vera/vitamin E, whatever, to cool it down for the next couple of days. But it's worth it, all the crap and dead skin is taken off your face and you do look like you've had 14 hours of sleep. It's great, everyone should do a course.

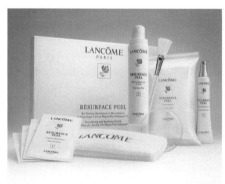

This kit is really good, though. Obviously containing a lower level of active ingredients than the salon version, it still contains enough to make a visible, but much gentler, difference. Simple to use, and everything is included. Use it a couple of times a week for a month, and *violà*!

Vichy Normaderm Clearer Skin Renovating System

This is a really, really simple kit to use, as everything is numbered in the order that you're supposed to use it, so it's totally idiot proof. Meant for use once a week for three weeks, all of the products are packaged in individual sachets and pouches in generous proportions. Plus, the aftercare moisturiser contains an SPF 15, which is vital when using a MDA product – your newly revealed skin is so sensitive at this time. Like the rest of the Normaderm range, this quite simply works.

Top Tip: Don't confuse glycolic peels with anything more severe (like dermal peels, for example). They're really mild and you can go straight into work afterwards.

beautfan

I had a Crystal Clear one about two weeks ago – they seem similar but I don't remember a mask at the end of my one. I really liked it and I almost fell asleep as I found the pressing of the wand quite relaxing. I didn't get a tingly sensation at all and didn't have a red face at the end of it either. I thought I looked about five years younger.

Cleopatra

I get up at half five most mornings to go to work and am normally bleary eyed at that hour. After about two weeks of using the Resurface kit, I looked in the mirror at 05.30, and lo and behold, the first thing I thought was, wow my skin looks really good this morning. It seemed clearer and brighter than usual. I am well impressed with this product, and would definitely recommend it.

GLYCOLIC PEEL

This really works. I can honestly say that the course of glycolic peels I had was the best thing I've ever done for my skin. I had lots of those little bumps under my skin – you know the kind that are impossible to get rid off? I'd tried everything but they just weren't shifting. For me, clearing up areas of congestion was the main reason for getting the peels done, but if ageing and fine lines are your concern, glycolics (like microdermabrasion) will lift off the surface layer of skin, making fine lines appear reduced and leaving your complexion much fresher.

Harto

I have had a course of six glycolic facials and peels and I can't believe the difference they made to my skin. Now I have one every six to eight weeks and my skin is behaving itself wonderfully.

I think I had about five peels. On the first couple there were no ill effects whatsoever – no redness, nothing to tell I'd had the peel done at all. On the third and fourth, though, I did break out. I had so many spots on my chin I could have warned ships off the coast. But after that – nothing. My skin cleared and stayed that way. Now I have a glycolic every once in a while to keep things smooth and clear.

The peel takes a surprisingly short time – it's timed by the second or the minute. The product is applied to your face with a brush. You may feel areas of tingling or slight stinging and the therapist will cool these down for you. Plus it's great if you get a little tube to hold (like a Hoover hose) to blow cold air on your face if you feel too warm. The peel is removed with a soothing cleanser, and moisturiser finishes the whole treatment off.

Top Tip: Many salon facials can incorporate a glycolic peel into the treatment. Ask about it when you're booking.

TEDDY BOBBS LIKES LANCÔME RESURFACE PEEL

Now if ye think these fancy glycolic peels are going to do some good, off ye go. But I'm telling you, they cost an absolute fortune and you can say goodbye to getting into something like an index-linked fund. Which admittedly hasn't been a great investment lately…

What would make much more sense is this kit here by Lancôme – Resurface Peel.

Ah listen, sure I know it's the truth that the home versions of a salon treatment can be a bit shite (pardon my French).

This one's different though, boy. It has a lower level of active ingredients than the salon version, but it will still do a good job. So if ye want to hang on to what's left of your SSIA, one of these kits will cost ye less than a salon treatment. Sound financial sense.

FACE MASKS

Is there any real benefit to using a mask, I hear you ask? Oh, you betcha. As skin ages, it thins, and that can lead to that papery effect. We've also got to contend with a loss of tone, increased pigmentation and the appearance of lines and wrinkles. Phew! So a good mask can be a very effective weapon in the anti-ageing battle, providing immediate lifting, brightening and hydrating benefits to the skin. Your buzzwords when picking out a mask should be things like 'toning', 'lifting' and 'firming'.

Great Face Masks

Chanel Sublimage Masque

It's very expensive, and darn it, it's very good. Chanel's Sublimage Masque is extremely nourishing and brilliant for super-dry complexions. Plus, if you bring it on holliers with you, you'll really see a difference if you use it after a day in the sun. Great stuff altogether.

Clarins Beauty Flash Balm

Good old Clarins Beauty Flash Balm is a brilliant tube of goodness to keep on hand when things are looking a bit dull and tired. Great for reviving hungover skin, it also provides a smooth cushion for make-up, meaning your foundation won't tend to sit deep into lines and wrinkles – and hey presto, you'll look younger. You can also use Flash Balm as a treatment – slap a thick layer on, lie down for 15 minutes and tissue off the excess.

Skin Wisdom Peel Peel Off Face Mask

Head to Tesco to pick up one of their best-kept beauty secrets – Skin Wisdom by Bharti Vyas. An expert facialist, her products are cheap as chips but really, really good. Try the Peel Off Face Mask, part of the Age Reverse line.

Elemis Pro-collagen Quartz Lift Mask

Comforting and nourishing, Elemis Pro-Collagen Quartz Lift Mask is a creamy formulation that helps to uplift skin, helping with sags and bags – and it's lovely and moisturising too.

4

Body Rock

People tend to go mad moisturising their faces but can sadly neglect their body moisturiser...

Sunscreen

Unfortunately, we don't live in the kind of climate where I need to exhort you all to slip, slap and slop at every opportunity. (Is it just me, or does that phrase make you think it's referring to some weird sexual practice? OK, it's just me then.)

But when the sun does come out (once in 1996 for six days straight and again in 2001 for two days in May), we are absolute hoors for it. We can't get enough. Out we go, discarding every inch of the clothing covering our lily-white bodies, throwing modesty to the wind. Disgusting beer bellies that should quite frankly be ashamed of themselves are proudly displayed to the dismayed public.

You don't need to be as fussy regarding sensitivity to body sunscreens as you do with your face. Faces are exposed to the sun all day long and skin here is much more sensitive. Body skin is tougher and responds well to most sunscreen brands. Go for the highest factor you can to protect against sun damage – you can always fake up your colour.

Irish people need at least a factor 20–30 on their bodies during exposure to summer sun. If you're hitting the Costas or other sunny climes, you'll need a higher level of sun protection – if you're very pale, go for a 50.

Kids and people with fair or sun-reactive skin need factor 50. Those spray-on sunscreens are fantastic for kids and boyfriends/husbands who won't put on sunscreen. But lads, come on. It's not very macho to get sunburn and have to lie in the holiday apartment covered in yoghurt while the rest of the gang parties all night without you, is it?

So apply sunscreen at a high factor – and apply it generously. You don't get the proper level of protection if you skimp on the quantity. Reapply every couple of hours and every time you've been in the water.

Don't go near products like P20. They stop you from burning, but they won't protect you against skin ageing and skin cancer.

Great Picks for Sunscreen

I love Boots Soltan, Vichy Capital Soleil, Ambre Solaire and Lancaster. All are great ranges and are constantly improving, not to mention tried and trusted.

Boots Soltan

The Boots Soltan range is great because it's so easy to use – the SPF and star rating make the products a cinch to understand. There is a range of factors up to 50 available, as well as products for kids.

Vichy Capital Soleil

Vichy is great for all sorts of reasons: good science, prices and formulations make their skincare lines hard to beat, and their Capital Soleil range of suncare products is equally as effective. Protection is offered up to factor 50 and you can choose from milks, fluids and sticks, depending on your preference.

Lancaster

Lancaster is my number-one for posh sun protection, providing a luxurious experience that's kind to skin, too. Protection from factor 15 to 50 is available, with UVA and UVB shielding.

Also Recommended: RoC Minesol and La Roche-Posay Anthelios.

MAMMY SAYS

Wait till I tell ye what it used to be like. This was in the days before global warming, when we used to get proper summers. Why the feck is it called global warming anyways? It's done nothing but lash since it was invented. We'd go off to Tramore with our tin foil held up to our faces, a bottle of Hawaiian Tropic sun oil and a deck chair. Hang sangwiches for the beach and a bottle of TK red lemonade. Lovely stuff.

Now we have cheap flights and we can go off furrin, of course. And do you know the girls have been telling me all about factor this and UVA that. I don't usually see the point to their mad newfangled ways, but this makes a lot of sense to me. It's no more tan oil for me.

Tina

I recently bought the Dr. Hauschka Sunscreen Cream for Children (for myself). It is a mineral sun protection, and contains ingredients such as rose petal, quince seed extract, rosehip seed, almond oil and seabuckthorn oil.

Gracie

I love Soltan. It's never let me down, is very nourishing on my skin and I love the smell. Piz Buin is another favourite.

BUT WHAT DOES ALL THE SCIENCE MEAN?

This is one that confuses the hell out of everyone, so I think we most definitely need a guide to sunscreens and the lingo they employ.

Chemical Sunscreen

These absorb the harmful UV radiation that comes from the sun. Chemical sunscreens can be UVA or UVB absorbers.

Physical Sunscreen

These physically block the sun's rays and deflect away both UVA and UVB radiation. Common physical blockers include titanium dioxide and zinc oxide, and they can often be quite thick and white.

UVA and UVB

UV wha? It's ultraviolet radiation from the sun (or sunbeds), and there are two main types:

- **UVA:** These rays accelerate the ageing process and are also a cancer risk.
- **UVB:** These are the rays that cause you to burn and also affect ageing and are a cancer risk. Basically, you need to avoid them both.

SPF and Stars

We all know that SPF stands for sun protection factor, but did you know that it applies *only* to UVB rays? You need to make sure the sunscreen protects against UVA too. The SPF number refers to the product's ability to block out the sun's burning rays and it is calculated by measuring the burn rate on unprotected skin. The higher the SPF, the greater the sun protection.

Coco

Hamilton Sports 30 is the best suncream I've found and I've tried loads over the years. You are supposed to reapply after four hours, but it's water resistant, just in case it actually gets warm enough for a beach day! It doesn't make you turn white but white flecks will show up in photos – but the flecks are actually what reflects the rays. And it's easy to apply.

The star rating indicates the amount of protection against UVA rays. Not all companies use this system, but the Boots Soltan range does, and we'd recommend it as a well-priced all-rounder.

THE ONE TO BUY

Most good sun creams will contain a mixture of physical and chemical suncreams. Get good at reading the ingredients and go for ones that incorporate zinc oxide or titanium dioxide.
You need to get a broad-spectrum (UVA and UVB) sunscreen with a SPF of at least 15.

AFTERSUN

After you've been exposed to the sun, you'll need to be reaching for that bottle of aftersun. Aftersun really does differ from normal body moisturiser, so make sure you use one of these special products. They contain ingredients to soothe and calm sun-scorched skin, prevent peeling (ugh) and put back the moisture that the sun has blasted out.

GREEN AND GORGEOUS:
Lavera After Sun Lotion

Lavera After Sun Lotion is one product I won't leave for foreign parts without, and one of the main reasons for this is the husband's surprising *grá* for it.

On holiday, I discovered that he, rooting around in my case for some aftersun, had found the Lavera and was liberally slathering it on. 'What's this stuff?' he asked. 'It's really nice and creamy. Smells like sweets.'

Now in case you're underwhelmed by this endorsement, let me first explain something. Never before has he volunteered an unprompted opinion on any product. I was so shocked I nearly fell off the bed, where I was reclining après our day poolside.

It's flippin' fantastic: rich, creamy, cooling, nourishing. Shea butter and sweet almond oil make this organic product an absolute must.

Best Budget Choice

Yucky packaging, but Fruit of the Earth's Skin Cooling Aloe Vera Lotion is brilliantly priced and great at cooling reddened skin. You can even get a spray-on version that's ace at getting to hard-to-reach areas. Keep it in the fridge for extra cooling power.

Top Tip: If you've overdone it, run a cool bath, sprinkle oatmeal into it and immerse yourself in it. Moisturising and skin soothing, this is a DIY trick that works.

Top Tip: If things are really bad on the burns front, wipe red areas with a face cloth soaked in milk – the lactic acid in cow juice soothes and repairs damaged skin.

Aftersun Enhancers and Prolongers

Another great idea is aftersun products with tan enhancer. Great results have been reported to me from the likes of Nivea, Ambre Solaire and other inexpensive brands. They tend to be a bit runny, so avoid if you want a rich, creamy experience. Of course, there's not much magic here – they're basically aftersun creams with a bit of fake tan mixed in.

WORK OF SATAN: Sunbeds and Sunlamps

You knew I was going to say this, didn't you? Despite the protestations of the sunbed industry, sunbeds are not safe. They blast out harmful concentrations of both UVA and UVB rays. They will prematurely age your skin and could increase your chance of developing skin cancer.

Ah listen, it's up to you. If you want to look like a dried-up crone well before your time, off you go. But I would seriously advise you to have a titter of wit and get a spray tan.

SCRUB UP

I'm very fond of scrubs and all manner of body exfoliation and I particularly like salt scrubs. They're honest and do the job they say they will. A sea salt-based scrub has the added benefit of actually drawing some toxins out of the skin.

They're particularly useful post-epilation (allowing trapped hairs to spring free) and pre-fake tanning (sloughing away dead skin to get a smooth, even colour). A great salt scrub will have gorgeous oils to moisturise and leave your skin soft and nourished. Plus it should smell terrific.

Great Picks for Scrubs

These are the ones I rate, and read on below to see what the Beaut.ies have found to be brilliant buys, too.

Origins Incredible Spreadable Scrub

Step up Origins Incredible Spreadable Scrub. Simply scrumptious, but don't do what Kirstie did and come home from the pub half cut and stick your tongue into this salt scrub to see if it tastes as nice as it smells. It doesn't.

Soap & Glory Flake Away

Cute packaging and super-effective scrubbing capabilities make Soap & Glory's Flake Away Spa Body Polish a powerhouse of a sugar scrub. A deadly price and great smell don't hurt, either.

Kirstie
Guinot's Smoothing Body Scrub is what I'm attacking scaly, wobbly upper arms and décolleté with. Effective but not painful – which I do find some salt or sugar scrubs can be – it doesn't leave skin reddened and sore. Instead, it gives you lovely smooth, soft skin which feels moisturised.

minxinparis
Another good one to try is L'Oréal Exfotonic, good value for money with excellent results.

Nikki
Exfotonic – it's brilliant. TIGI Oatmeal Cookie Sugar Scrub is gorgeous, good enough to eat and when applied to skin, goes hot. It's fab, but a bit expensive!

Tinkerbell

My fave exfoliant has to be L'Occitane's almond body scrub. It smells fab and you feel like you're really pampering yourself!

cathyfly

I like the Sanctuary salt scrub too and I've also been known to use the St Ives facial scrub all over as a budget option! I don't like the scrubs with oil in them as I find they leave skin too greasy … prefer to moisturise afterwards. I got a fab Nue Blue Eriu hamper recently with products from a brand called Daniele De Winter which I'd never heard of before and it had a fabulous body scrub in it which I'm definitely buying again. I got a body lotion and cellulite oil from the same brand and they are both really nice too.

Sanctuary Spa Essentials Body Scrub

Sanctuary Spa Essentials Body Scrub is great for before lashing on the self-tanner, and is often available in three-for-two offers, which makes it nice and affordable – and sure, we like a bit of that.

Yes to Carrots Moisturizing Body Scrub

Yes to Carrots Moisturizing Body Scrub is a squeezable tube of antioxidant-packed goodness that's best kept for delicate areas like the chest, as it's not quite heavy-duty enough to deal with serious scales.

Top Tip: Apply your scrub of choice to dry skin, and rub in hard – stand on a bathmat or in the shower when you do this, as it can get messy – then shower off. It makes the product much more effective.

Top Tip: If you use a product with oil, it'll take the place of a body moisturiser, meaning there's no need to use a separate product, which will save you time.

SALON BODY SCRUBS AND POLISHES

Now, these are a big favourite of mine. I love getting scrubbed and buffed to within an inch of my life by a therapist using a heavy-duty salon brand. All the bits you couldn't reach yourself – like your back – are exfoliated and smoothed by the therapist.

The scrubs and polishes used in salons or spas are usually completely luxurious and will often have different formulas to suit the different skin types. Shower the scrub off and the therapist will apply a body moisturiser or body butter. You will feel totally gorgeous afterwards.

Top Tip: A salon scrub is a brilliant first step for a spray or home tan – just make sure you get it done the day before so any oils used have a chance to absorb properly.

Golden Body Treatment

A therapy with the real Midas touch. A golden body treatment is a fantastic twist on the normal scrub/moisturising routine. I had this done in the heavenly Inchydoney Island Spa. A totally blissful experience, it started off with a milky, moisturising Cleopatra bath followed by a body scrub. A golden shimmering body lotion is then applied, bringing colour and sparkle to your skin. So fantastic for big night out (or big night in …), though as I was there with a gaggle of girlfriends I had to be content to shimmer inside my dress with only my arms on show.

REN Guerande

Fresh, pepperminty and moisturising balm that's a luxurious pick-me-up. It's also fab to use before a spray tan.

Also Recommended: Biotherm Lait de Gommage, Clinique Sparkle Skin.

TEDDY BOBBS ADVISES

Hmmmm, now I've one thing to say to anyone who buys these fancy scrub yokes. It'll do nothing for your bottom line. Financial bottom line, that is. A bit of scrub on the arse might do wonders for your real bottom line. Ahem ... now where was I? Ah yeah, a recipe for yis now.

DIY: Olive Oil and Sea Salt Scrub

It's so simple to make your own body scrub and many people prefer them. Mix up sea salt and oil to make a paste, and that's it! Exfoliating and skin softening in one. You can add a drop or two of your favourite aromatherapy oil to the paste if you like, to make it smell delish.

If you rub this onto your skin and leave it for a minute or two before showering off, you'll give the sea salt a chance to work its skin detoxifying magic.

Japanese Washcloths

What're these now, when they're at home? Popular in, you guessed it, Japan, they tend to be made from a loosely woven synthetic material and can be used all over the body. They help your shower gel last longer too, as a small amount will foam up really well using the cloth. And you can throw them in the washing machine if they get a bit pongy too. I tip the nod to Space NK and Muji's versions. Very good now altogether.

BODY MOISTURISING

People tend to go mad moisturising their faces but can sadly neglect their body moisturiser. If we're spending money, we just don't want to spend it on body moisturiser, do we? Not when there are gorgeous products for the face and make-up to die for. Thankfully, this is another area where less expensive products really do work and you can happily substitute away if you want to.

And if you want to splash out   oh, what a treat awaits you. Those super-duper body moisturisers are really fantastic. Clinique's Deep Comfort line and Estée Lauder's body products are really good buys. Estée Lauder would always be my choice for body firming creams. Yum. Their Body Performance Firming Body Creme is just fab. Expensive, yes, but worth it.

But whatever you do choose, make sure you slather it on good and proper. Always use your moisturiser after your baths and showers – your skin will thank you for it and tell you so by becoming smoother, softer and more supple.

Beautygeek

I also use sweet almond oil/coconut oil/olive oil with finely milled salt. I use a wind-dried (not in tumble dryer) face cloth, as it dries to a rough texture, and I then use it with my normal facial cleanser … I don't see the point in spending lots for something that I could make up myself!

xgirl

Have you tried using a Japanese washcloth in the shower? Muji sells them and they make such a difference to my skin with regular use. And much easier to use than a separate scrub – you just use them like a normal sponge with your shower gel.

The type of body moisturiser you go for, of course, depends on your skin type and how much moisture you like. Me, I love body butters and rich creams. You might be a lighter, lotion type of gal. So here are my top picks and we'll also see what everyone else loves to give us a bit of inspiration.

Top Six Rich Body Moisturisers

Loved for their ability to smell great as well as being powerful enough to improve a piece of bark (or scaly pins), these gorgeous moisturisers are a daily treat and most won't break the bank.

Body Shop Body Butters

Yum. Simply yum. These guys come in tons of flavours, use fairtrade ingredients and always smell wonderful. We're big fans at Beaut.ie.

Seapig

I love L'Occitane Supple Skin Oil, the almond one … smells gorgeous and leaves your skin really soft. Their grape body moisturiser is lovely too. Another favourite is the Neutrogena Body Oil, really light, especially if you put it on when you're just out of the shower and then towel-dry yourself.

Elizabeth Arden Eight Hour Cream Intensive Moisturizing Body Treatment

A natural progression of her famous Eight Hour Cream, the body lotion isn't so heavily scented, but is a thick, silky cream that works wonders on dry skin.

Palmer's Cocoa Butter

An old reliable, you might remember this one from your childhood. Found in every chemist in the land, it's a good price and does a good job of descaling skin too. And if you're a fan of the smell of cocoa butter, sure that's just a bonus.

Vaseline Cocoa Butter

Available in a body butter or a conditioning lotion, these products perform and are available at a great price, too.

Yes to Carrots Deliciously Rich Body Butter

If you're not a fan of baby powder scents, then you may not like this, but you will like how wonderfully well it soothes sore, stressed skin. Brilliant for wintertime, apply at night before bed and wake up with silky-smooth pins, bum and tum.

Also Recommended: Nivea Soft, L'Occitane Shea Butter Ultra Rich Body Cream and Cien Body Butter at Lidl.

ladyelvis
I tried the new Neutrogena dry skin moisturiser and it's very nice, I must say. But I always go back to the Nivea Body Moisturiser for dry skin … lovely.

Connie
I've been using the auld reliable Vaseline lotion in a yellow bottle since my teens. I've tried lots of others too (Dove, Nivea, St Ives), but always went back to Vaseline, cos it soaks into skin the quickest, it's not sticky and I don't have to wait for it to dry before throwing on the clothes.

LA ROCHE-POSAY ISO-UREA

Iso-Urea is rich and thick and is a body lotion that makes your skin feel like velvet and actually gently exfoliates while it's at it. Despite concerns by some that the name is a bit reminiscent of pee, it smells gorgeous. Give your skin a treat and give it some Iso-Urea. Buy it in good chemists.

girlfriday

Really like La Roche-Posay body lotion – smells faintly of roses and is very effective. Am currently in the middle of a delicious Ginger Souffle body lotion from Origins – smells so good you could eat it!

Gracie

I'm using a body creme, came in a tub, by Cien from Lidl and its quite impressive for its price. Has a smell similar to the Nivea cucumber one and has a lovely light, whipped texture that moisturises nicely. I've also a large tub of Eucerin on hand for the auld flaky patches on the upper arms. Other favourites include Lush Dream Cream, Body Shop Shea Butter and Nivea Q10.

BODY SPRAYS AND LOTIONS

But here, what if you're not in the mood for a thick, rich cream? For instance, say you have to put a pair of tights on straight away – sure, you'd be shagged, so check out a dry oil instead. I like Espa's Nourishing Body Oil, which can be sprayed on, rubbed in and tights can be slinked up immediately. It's a bit expensive though, so check out Soap & Glory's sweet-smelling (and purse-friendly) Flirtigo Body Moisturizing Mist instead.

Keratosis Pilaris — Goosebump Arms

The problem: Agh, this is a pain-in-the-ass problem – little bumps on your upper arm that no amount of body brushing or scrubbing seems to shift. Men can suffer equally from the dreaded bumps. Keratosis pilaris is caused by the hair follicles in the skin on the upper arm getting blocked by an excess of the protein keratin. These harden and form 'plugs'. Usually confined to the upper arms, keratosis pilaris can also occur on legs.

As well as looking yuck, they can also leave you feeling like you're in an episode of the *Itchy and Scratchy* show. And because the hair follicle is blocked, you might also suffer from ingrown hairs in the area.

The solution: All I want is smooth arms, you wail. So what to do? Well, there's a standout product that might just be the answer you're looking for. It's by Eucerin, and it's called Intensive 10% w/w Urea Treatment Lotion.

PinkPanther
Eucerin is a true miracle cream. I had been plagued by keratosis pilaris my whole life and tried everything – including strange herbal tablets. Nothing worked until someone on the blather recommended this last year.

Jennifer
What a miracle, I started using this cream last week and I've got new arms! It's quite a thick cream but is very silky as well. It doesn't smell and my bumpy arms were unbelievably smooth after one day and a week later the bumps are gone … it's a miracle cream. I won't ever be without it.

Lynnie
I've found something that really shifts the blighters. It's Eucerin's Intensive 10% w/w Urea Treatment Lotion. It moisturises and softens dry, rough skin, and it works. Applied twice daily, my keratosis pilaris was substantially less noticeable from day one and was just about gone completely by day three. Magic!

gingersnap

I was in Brown Thomas Saturday afternoon and they had a mini catwalk set up modelling swimwear. All the models were really slim and tall, and I took enormous pleasure in noticing that even some of them had cellulite.

Bee

The Body Shop Cellulite Serum is great. They have a great massager that's like the body brush. Gets the circulation going. The serum is minty and makes your skin tingle. Remember, cellulite isn't really about your weight. It's got more to do with drainage of impurities.

Gracie

Definitely body brushing, L'Oréal Perfect Slim and wearing my MBTs! Honestly they have really helped tone up my legs and derrière region!

CELLULITE

Cellulite is the bane of most women's lives. Everyone has it, except, perhaps, Olympic athletes and Wimbledon contenders. The reason models in magazines don't look as though they don't have any cellulite is because they've been airbrushed. It's nigh on impossible to shift, so don't beat yourself up about it.

While I've only ever encountered a couple of products I've seen noticeable results with, there are products out there with active ingredients like caffeine, which is used to stimulate the blood flow. The theory is that when blood rises up to below the surface of the skin, it takes the nasty toxins that cause cellulite away with it. I'm sceptical, and feel that no topical product for this problem works on its own. By all means use an anti-cellulite product, but combine it with body brushing and a good diet that's rich in the nutrients found in fruits, veg and eggs. Then you'll see a difference, but like anything worth doing in life, it'll take a bit of effort.

L'Oréal Perfect Slim

I'm not sure whether it's the action of the cream or the fact that you have to follow a set of steps, but this product really encourages you when you're starting a new routine, because it gives you massage techniques to follow, and those plus the ingredients in the cream do help with the dreaded orange peel.

Clarins High Definition Body Lift

Really nice and firming, this has a two-step approach. Skin firmness is addressed, which helps immediately, and Clarins has used lots of nice botanical goodies to help break down fatty tissue. Just make sure you use firm massage strokes and you should see results. Plus the name Total Body Lift fills me with hope.

Let's see what's worked for everyone else.

BODY BRUSHING

There's no doubt about it – body brushing is a Very Good Thing. It's easy, it's cheap and it requires only a leetle bit of effort on the part of a lazy personage.

Why Should I Do It?

The skin is the biggest organ of elimination in the body and brushing can speed up the elimination of toxins. Benefits can include improved circulation, increased lymphatic drainage, smoother skin and – this is key – a reduction in cellulite. Plus it's also great for preventing ingrown hairs and even keratosis pilaris (those annoying little bumps on your arms).

Sheryl
Endermologie did NOT work at all for me. It made my cellulite worse! I had about 13 sessions, had purchased 20 … I didn't get my money back but was afraid to finish it out. I'm going to look into yoga, which I hear really helps.

girlfriday
One great anti-cellulite product is the iconic Fat Girl Slim by Bliss. I have certainly noticed a big improvement when using this product in conjunction with MBT shoes. I don't know if it is the product or the shoes, but the combination certainly works. I don't think any product on its own can be a magic cure for the dreaded cellulite. You really need to body brush and work those ass muscles to see any difference.

How Do I Body Brush?

So how exactly should you do it to reap these rewards? As confusion often reigns about this procedure, I've assembled a handy four-step How-To.

1. Start with dry skin, before your bath or shower. Wet skin can stretch and pull and you won't get the benefit of brushing away those dead auld skin cells.

2. Beginning with the soles of your feet, brush upwards towards your heart. Same with your arms – always brush towards your heart.

3. Brush your tummy in circular anti-clockwise strokes (to complement digestion).

4. Brush the boobage area very gently (avoid the nipples, as this would be a big ouch factor).

And you're done. This should take about two minutes before your morning shower and can have amazing results. You can buy body brushes in any big chemist or pharmacy. Body Shop brushes always come in for high praise and of course all the fancy-pants body ranges do their own. A long-handled brush makes things easier if you're a bit stiff and creaky and is of course ideal for reaching those hard-to-get at areas like the back.

Fabilis altogether, wha? Sure, you should be asking yourself at this point – why wouldn't I be brushing?

Errol's girl

Yep, the body brushing is great – it's just remembering to do it. But it does work. I used to get little bumps on my arms but they completely cleared after body brushing. Initially you'll get little spots, but then they go also. Have been using the new Nivea green gel stuff and to be honest haven't noticed any difference.

STRETCH MARKS

If you've had a baby or are a yo-yo dieter, chances are you'll be well acquainted with these feckers. And even if you've done neither of these things, it doesn't matter. Growing up can actually cause stretch marks. So much has been written about the causes of stretch marks and how to prevent them, and what it all boils down to is some folk are simply prone to them.

The best time to do something about them is when they're still red. After they've turned silvery, you might as well get to love them, as sad to say, they ain't going nowhere.

Murad does a fantastic Firm and Tone Serum, which is great for stretch marks, and of course you may want to give the famous StriVectin-SD a try. Developed to banish stretch marks, women began to use it on their faces too, giving it cult status as a multifunctional wonder that works.

Use every weapon in your armoury as soon as you discover you're pregnant to prevent them in the first place!

redmum

With regard to pregnancy and stretch marks, I think you are either prone to them or you aren't. I certainly had them by 32 weeks across my lower tummy. I would also hold my hand up and say I didn't smear enough on me to judge my last sweeping statement completely, but I know pregnant pals who did nothing and got nothing, if you know what I mean.

Sinead

Well I can report first-hand that I've been using a combination of:
a) Bio Oil
b) Mama Mio Tummy Rub Oil
c) Mama Mio Tummy Rub Stretch Mark Cream

And don't have a single stretch mark so far at 33 weeks, and I'm quite big for someone who's usually a size 8. (Swollen) fingers crossed it stays that way! So I reckon oils are better than creams …

dancing queen

The real danger time for stretch marks is around 36 weeks, so keep up the good work. Unfortunately I concentrated on my hip area and didn't pay attention to my belly button and they appeared before I even realised it! Now I am one of millions of women trying to find a cure! Not successful yet, but living in hope!

Red

The thing about these products and anti-cellulite creams etc. is that surely the action alone would make a difference. I think the creams are more of an incentive, unless you like to stroke your bust a lot …

Cherry

I think Red's right, it's the massage and the moisturisation that does the trick. I've got that Nivea Good-Bye Cellulite stuff and I do my bum, my thighs, my tum and my bust every day. Sad I know, but it seems to be working. And it's only ten quid.

NGO

Body Shop Vitamin E cream is great and good old Palmer's – the cocoa butter stretch mark massage cream is very good (apparently Catherine Zeta Jones swore by it when preggers!) – very cheap too!

Bust-firming Creams

A general air of despondency seems to hang in the air whenever the subject turns to bust-firming creams. Apart from the stand-out Pout Bustier, which is sadly no longer with us, I've never heard anyone say that any of these creams work. So I have no definitive product recommendations here, but a generous application of firming body creams can't do any harm!

Diet Away Your Cellulite

It's more or less universally agreed that a healthy diet plays a huge part in shifting cellulite. This means less coffee, booze, ciggies, stodge. And tight jeans.

The more sedentary you are, i.e. the more time you spend sitting on your arse every day, the worse your cellulite will be. You need to get the blood flowing, the lymph glands draining and pump those lungs full of fresh air.

Now I'm a fine one to talk – I'm just telling you what the experts say. God knows I couldn't give up my morning coffee if you paid me. And if you were to cut out everything else as well, a cellulite-free life seems … a bit boring.

But I do try to detox when I've been very very bad.

DETOX

Detoxing is a subject we're always fascinated by, twice a year in particular: post-Christmas and post-holidays.

The song remains the same every Crimbo, doesn't it? You've eaten like a little porky pig, snaffling every treat available. Whoever invented the goddamn tin of Roses needs to be hauled up before a court for crimes against waistlines. And you just couldn't leave that delicious ham alone, could you? What was it doing, calling to you from the fridge? And you've drunk Far Too Much. There's no need for you to feel a single-handed responsibility to diminish the EU's wine lakes.

So in the best Irish tradition of feeling hugely guilty after a binge, you resolve to purge. You can't fit into your jeans and your backside looks like bubble wrap. Serious measures need to be taken. Only spring water and salads will pass your lips, you're going to go to the gym every day and sign up for a slimming club.

Yeah right, I believe you …

COLONICS

Princess Diana undeniably brought this treatment to the attention of the masses. We discovered that she preferred to get gallons of water flushed up her bum every week instead of just doing a poo like the rest of us.

But as claims of quite dramatic weight loss and reduction in bloating etc. were made, people became more attuned to the idea. But they were still saying, 'I'm never getting that done – no way!' Now when people say that to me, I know it's definitely a case of the lady doth protest too much and that they're secretly dying to get it done. See also: Botox.

Colonic treatments are shrouded in mystery, so Beaut.ie embarked on an investigation into the murky world of colonics. We wanted to find out what having a colonic hydrotherapy treatment was really like. Is it uncomfortable? Is it embarrassing? Do you really feel healthier afterwards? And the million-dollar question – do you lose any weight?

A lot of people like the idea of the quick detox, the promise of weight loss and the lighter, cleaner feeling a colonic is purported to bring. But on the other hand … well, it *is* a hose of water up your bum.

Urban legend has it that colonics can flush out all sorts of undigested truths, from the piece of Lego swallowed twenty years earlier to the unchewed food you gulped down a week ago. God knows what's lurking inside us all. It has to be good to flush out stuff like that … doesn't it?

I've heard quite a few positive reports about colonics. Apparently it's not embarrassing in the slightest. The only awkward moment came when someone arrived for her appointment at the colonic clinic only to be told that it would have to be rescheduled because the drains were blocked. When she told me, I couldn't stop laughing. The irony! And the poor bloody plumber.

Anyway, back to business. My advice: don't embark on a session of colonics to lose weight, but rather to kick-start a healthier lifestyle. Everyone agrees that one of the most helpful aspects of the treatment is the nutritional advice given by the therapists.

Now, like any alternative health treatment, you must fully research this whole process before you decide to have it done yourself. The jury is still most definitely out on this one and the mainstream medical establishment doesn't agree with it at all, plus you will have to take a course of good-gut-bacteria afterwards, as the water flushes everything out, good and bad. But if you're happy to go ahead, you might find it useful as a starting point to a healthy new regime.

CELEBRITY BEAUTY SECRETS:
The Butt Facial

No, I'm not kidding. Salons in Beverly Hills (where else?) began to give facials – on the arses of their pampered clients. Then the trend took off and quickly spread to other salons and clinics throughout the States.

Bums are exfoliated and cleansed, then there's a thorough pummelling with a cellulite-reducing machine. A mask is applied while head and feet are massaged and – this is the best bit – extractions are performed if necessary. So in other words, big red pimples are squeezed – ugh! Then comes the waxing – *ripppppppp*!

Now you can also choose a butt lift, where the bum is tightened and lifted by the treatments. Or you can get microdermabrasion on your bum. And some salons finish with a spray tan.

BODY WRAPS

I usually adore body wraps, the ones where you're slathered in some lovely goo or mud, covered in tin foil and left to snooze on a heated bed for half an hour. Any beauty treatment requiring absolutely no effort whatsoever on the part of *moi* always gets a big thumbs up.

But when I tried an inch-loss wrap complete with mummy-style bandages, I hated it. 'You'll lose inches,' the therapist promised, taking an assortment of slimy-looking bandages out of a bucket. 'This wrap is great for detox too, the seaweed softens skin and improves circulation, so it helps cellulite.'

All good to hear. Clad only in the paper knickers, first I had to subject myself to getting every bit of myself measured and the therapist recorded it all in a little notebook (waist 23" etc.). Then I was wrapped up in said green slimy bandages. I lay down on a heated bed yoke and was covered in foil. I liked this part of the treatment, as it meant lovely warm snooze time. Plus I got a head massage at the end of it.

All too soon, it was back on my feet to be unwrapped. The bandages were unwound, I showered off the slime and then it was time to be measured again.

'You've lost seven inches,' the therapist announced brightly. Hmmm, I wasn't really convinced.

I didn't like this treatment at all, although I know some people adore it. It's a perennial feature of spa menus, so it must be popular. It just wasn't for me, I suppose. And when I put my jeans back on, they were still too tight.

Bee

Aha, I did this a few years ago and was very doubtful. I was only too happy to lounge around reading magazines, but it did make me feel like a mummy. I ended up losing some inches off my wrists and ankles. Needless to say, I didn't go back.

GornGal

Do you think they could just wrap your tummy and get the seven inches off there?

Gloss

I had the Universal Contour Wrap a few years ago. When it was finished and all the inches counted, it seemed that I lost inches from skinny places like my arms, and lost nothing from my more, em, generously padded areas, like my bum. I wonder if it is harder to extract fluid from the fatty areas of your body? However, there was one really good result – I've had stretch marks since I was 11 and they were totally tightened up and contracted for a few days. I may not have had a bikini bod at the end of it, but I was a lot happier with the appearance of my hips and thighs at the end of it.

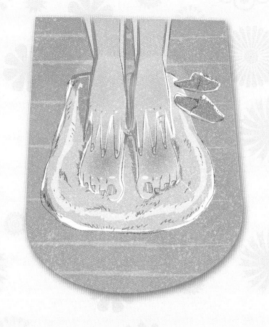

5

Paws and Claws

THE SHINE, THE HEALTH AND THE FEEL OF NATURAL BUFFED NAILS WITHOUT POLISH IS FANTASTIC...

HAND CREAM

I have a passion for hand cream. As soon as I see a new one, I just have to have a go. I leave it beside every sink in the house, on my bedside table and on my desk at work. If you do the same, you will soon notice colleagues sidling up for 'a chat' and borrowing an aul' slick of hand cream while they're there. I will use any old cream for work purposes (particularly for work, as anything nice I leave on my desk gets swiped). Look out for two-for-one offers in the supermarket and chemists. Vaseline, Nivea and Olay all do good ones. A great one for work is Yes to Carrots – it never seems to run out.

Most of the quality cosmetic companies all do decent ones, and hand cream is another area where less expensive options can be terrific. Look out for SPF protection as an added bonus to protect against sun ageing. This can really raise the price, though, so as a cheaper alternative try letting your hand cream sink in, then applying a high-factor suncream.

Great Picks for Hands

AISLING'S PICK

My absolute favourite is Elizabeth Arden Eight Hour Cream Intensive Moisturizing Hand Treatment. It sinks right in, is velvety smooth and leaves your hands soft and plumped up instantly.

Boots Amazon Forest Passion Flower and Cupuaçu Hand & Nail Cream

Rich and fruity and perfect for your kitchen windowsill.

Yes to Carrot's Hand and Elbow Moisturizing Cream

Put this on your desk at work and expect to never, ever see it again, so hide it in a drawer instead. Yes to Carrot's stellar Hand and Elbow Moisturizing Cream is a budget wonder that quite simply works.

L'Occitane Shea Butter Hand Cream

L'Occitane's fab Shea Butter Hand Cream is packed full of super-duper-moisturising goodies and is the one to turn to for sore, chapped hands. You can use it overnight too for extra conditioning goodness.

GREEN AND GORGEOUS:
Dr. Hauschka Hand Cream

There are a lot of natural hand creams on the market. The most worthy of note is from good old Dr. Hauschka. His neem hand cream is incredibly rich. It smells divine, is creamy and nourishing and will leave your hands feeling fresh and soft. Use it in conjunction with the good doctor's Neem Nail Oil Pen and you've got yourself an unbeatable duo, Batman.

girlfriday

The Clarins Hand and Nail Treatment Cream is fab, but if your hands need some serious help, perhaps Neutrogena hand cream would be better. I recently got a tube of Kiehl's Ultimate Strength Hand Salve and I highly recommend it also, although it is difficult to get here (I got it in the States).

Kirstie

Estée Lauder Re-Nutriv hand cream is amazing, as is the Bliss lemon and bergamot one. They're the two I use.

Trinity

Aveeno hand cream. I've tried absolutely everything and started using this about two months ago. It doesn't 'hovvvvver' on your hands like some creams, but soaks right in and is great on the nails as well.

CELEBRITY CAUTIONARY TALE: Madonna Hands

Oh dear. Fantastic as she may be, with an absolutely amazing figure, Madonna's hands really let her down. *Tick tock, tick tock* – time doesn't go by slowly enough, it seems. Once you catch a glimpse of those bejewelled claws, you're left in no doubt as to her 'maturity'. And all the leotard-clad groin thrusting in the world ain't doing her any favours either. But that's another story.

When you take the decision, as she did, to preserve body over face, unfortunately hands also suffer, and they suffer more than the face does, it seems. Super-slim women like Sarah Jessica Parker also suffer from the claw hand syndrome. When you're faced with the battle of maintaining a size-zero figure and keeping your hands presentable, you're probably looking at injectibles to make a difference. For the rest of us (in the normal world), I'd advise tons and tons of hand cream.

Zinnie

I'm a complete hand cream addict – always have been. Yes to Carrots on the desk in work, which I constantly use because of the cheap-ass soap in our toilets. Estée Lauder Re-Nutriv in my handbag for any emergency use and Barielle Intensive Hand Treatment Cream for night-time – can't use the cotton gloves in bed though, way too creepy!

COTTON GLOVES FOR SUPER-SOFT HANDS

If your hands are really dry, try this. You know those little cotton gloves you've seen for overnight hand treatments? Well, they work! Slather your hands with cream and put on the gloves. When I first did this, I got a terrible slagging from my husband, who said it was like going to bed with Marcel Marceau. But don't listen to any remarks like this, because in the morning you'll be thrilled with the effect of your little white gloves.

The same principle works for feet. Go to bed with your feet slathered in foot cream, pop a pair of cotton socks on and the difference in the morning will be amazing. You can buy both at The Body Shop.

Ones to Try: Bliss Glamour Gloves

Bliss Glamour Gloves take the concept of overnight hand treatment all the way to heaven. In the words of Ned Flanders, these gloves are scrumdiddlyumptious.

In the words of Beaut.ie, they're fanfeckintastic.

Nylon gloves with a special gel lining, they 'force-feed' ceramides, grape seed, jojoba and olive oils plus antioxidants into your skin. You can super-charge the treatment by slathering on your own hand cream too, and they leave skin soft, silky and rehydrated after 20 minutes. You can use the gloves up to 50 times, and there are also socks in the range – ab fab.

Jill
I bought these for my mum for Crimbo and she is only delirah with them. She was all grumpy with me for using them when I was home with her until I told her you can buy a refill gel for them.

NOW HANDS THAT DO DISHES CAN FEEL AS SOFT AS YOUR FACE

Well, only if you wear rubber gloves, that is. They're a necessary evil if you do a lot of washing up/cleaning/putting your hands in water all day. The problem with rubber gloves, though, is that they can leave your hands a bit stinky and clammy, so replace them often.

Top Tip: Before you slip on your Marigolds, put on a nice rich hand cream and a pair of little cotton gloves. The hot water will act like a mini sauna on your hands, leaving them soft and gorgeous!

TEDDY BOBBS GOES FOR THE CUTICLE

When our financial advisor Teddy Bobbs saw this chapter, he was delira. 'Sure, there's milluns of things that can be done on the cheap to get your extremities looking good,' he enthused. 'And none of them require you giving up your eight cans of Coke a day habit that has the potential to drive your husband into a week-long bender.'

Excellent! And he's right, as usual. So here's a great recipe for cuticle oil to keep yourself gorgeous hand and feet wise.

DIY: Cuticle Oil

Lavishing your nails with cuticle oil is one of the best things you can do to keep your nails strong and healthy. To be honest, rubbing olive oil into your nails every night when you're watching the box works really well, so you might just like to try that instead. But if you're hell bent on making up a fancy pants oil, here's the recipe.

Get an old medicine or serum bottle – you know the kind, a tinted glass with a dropper. I use an empty Estée Lauder Advanced Night Repair bottle. You'll need:

- Sweet almond oil.
- Jojoba oil.
- Olive oil.
- Essential oil (any smell you love – citrus, lavender, ylang ylang or vanilla).

Mix the almond, jojoba and olive oils in equal parts and add a couple of drops of the essential oil (this is optional and just to make it smell even nicer). Keep in the fridge and make sure to rub into your nails every day.

FAVOURITE NAIL POLISH

Nail polish colours are an absolutely brilliant way to bring your look bang up to date. Without much outlay, you can easily keep up with trends. The more expensive, fashion-led brands like Chanel or Yves Saint Laurent will normally lead the way, but happily for us, salon and budget brands quickly jump on the bandwagon and copy the hottest colours of the season. So whether it's inky blue, plum, chocolate brown, day-glo pink or any other colour in between, I love to change colours and render even the most sober work outfit on-trend.

And if your boss isn't too keen on your Marilyn Manson-inspired black varnish? Keep it for the weekend and stay perfectly turned out with nude nails, which will never go out of fashion.

Chips don't show as easily, meaning maintenance isn't such a hassle. I'm a big fan of Pure Color varnishes from Estée Lauder for nude nails – great coverage, loads of subtle shades and they dry rock hard.

Candy Girl

Hello, Leighton Denny. We love you at Beaut.ie, and we love your range of high-shine shades too. His screamingly bright pinks, reds and oranges are brilliant with a tan, look great on toes and are the perfect antidote to winter weather.

Pink to Make the Boys Wink

Essie has a huge array of pink shades, all of which can be worn solo or as part of the ever-popular French mani. They're also strong on seasonal colours, so you'll always find a hard-to-locate shade within their collections.

Kirstie
I like Essie, I must say, and Leighton Denny. Rimmel's 60 Second polishes are fab.

Twinkletoes
I'm an Essie, OPI or Rimmel kind of girl. Rimmel for the cheapie last-minute option to match something, the others most of the time!

Dark and Dramatic

Ahh, OPI. Their Lincoln Park After Dark shade refuses to budge off polish bestseller lists and they're the ones to turn to for deep, dark, dramatic polishes.

Best Budget Polishes

Rimmel and Bourjois are hard to beat here. The fab fan-brush in Bourjois's 1 Seconde Nail Enamel coats in, well, one second, and Rimmel's 60 Seconds polish dries in, you guessed it, one minute. They do what they say on the tin, so.

Back to Base

A true can't-live-without product, the fantastic base coats by Jessica Nails will make an incredible difference to your nails. There are a few available, but Critical Care Basecoat & Topcoat for Soft Nails can be used alone as a treatment, or with polish to seal and protect nails. One gripe – they take *ages* to dry, but sure, I can live with that.

xgirl

Bourjois is fantastic for the price and has some great colours – their Cerise Noire is a great fake-it for Chanel Rouge Noir fans. I have been known to pick up a few Chanel polishes in duty free from time to time and have also ordered OPI from discount online sellers, but don't find the quality of the polish to be any better than Bourjois, so wouldn't pay full-price here.

HOW TO PAINT NAILS

If you're using a one-coat wonder from, say, Rimmel, Maybelline or Bourjois that's quick-drying, then generally, you can just lash it on and go. But if you're using a salon range like OPI or Essie, you need to follow a few guidelines to get the best out of them. These polishes are created with pro application in mind, and you'll be disappointed if you apply one coat and expect it to last – it won't. So, use a base coat, the two coats of polish (take the polish over the tip of the nail to help it last) and then seal the deal with a top coat. You should get a good five days from a paint job if you follow these steps.

Top Tip: Argh! I went outside the edges! Calm down, ladies, as Michael Winner might say. If you've made a hames of your hands, all is not lost. Get yourself some of Leighton Denny's Precision Colour Corrector, which comes with a wee brush and makes it a cinch to tidy up any messes you may make.

Top Tip: If nails are stained from brights or dark shades, lash them into a bowl of warm water you've added some bicarbonate of soda to. It'll clean them in a jiffy.

hockeysticks

I have to say I find if you put on an undercoat they all last much longer, even the cheapy ones … and for extra shine and 'toughness', a top coat is great too … but you also need a lot of time to let them dry properly. I love Rimmel, have a great MAC one – Vintage Vamp, I think – and I got some great cheapy ones in Superdrug last time I was in the UK … love them! I have an Essie super-dooper top coat … it's brillo.

Babaduck

I love Essie and OPI and if you buy online, they're as good value as the cheapo stuff you get here … and they're far more long-lasting. A decent base and top coat is also worth its weight in gold. Sally Hansen Mega Shine is pretty decent and I swear, swear, SWEAR by Tesco Make-Up's Goodbye Yellow nail treatment polish. Even worn alone, it gives your nails a lovely glow. Another good bargain range is Maybelline – the Express Finish range is fabilis for those in a hurry. I tried (and hated) the Bourjois 1 Seconde polish.

Bee

I've also tried black recently but you need really even-length nails to pull it off. Bought a little Mavala bottle of black as I didn't see the point in buying a bigger bottle, and it's great. My boss nearly died when I walked in with them, so I'll use the nude colours Mon–Fri and black at the weekend. It looked great on the toes, by the way!

Gel Nail Addiction

It's like they're a compulsion or something. Every time I got them done, I would promise myself it was the last time. They wreck your real nails for months afterwards, and let's face it – they just don't look real, do they?

And yet for ages I kept on doing it. I was possibly inspired by a cousin of mine who manages to look ridiculously glamorous with a full set of gels. If I was going to a big event, I would automatically think gel nails. But then the problems would start. I'd find them too long, or too thick, or they'd just look ridiculous. And I couldn't zip up my jeans, write anything down or send a text.

Try your best not to give in. Instead, nurture your nails with the right products and lavish care on them. Let them soak up cuticle oil and drink in base coats. Buy them pretty polish and seal the whole lot off with top coat. Don't go for instant gratification, because you have to live with the destruction for months afterwards.

Every time I write about this, I get angry comments or emails from nail technicians. It's because you're not getting them properly removed, they insist. It's because someone who isn't trained properly is putting them on in the first place. Nah-ah. To attach the gels, the natural nail must be deeply scored and damaged for the glue to adhere. I've tried this every which way but loose, and I can tell you that this kind of artificial nail is bad news.

Kelly

I got the gel nails for Crimbo cos my own were horrible, really weak/peely, not very nice. Got them off this week and it's cringe-worthy stuff. I can't button buttons, lace up me shoes, put on socks/trousers without my lickle butty nails folding back … honestly, they are like sheets of paper. I go weak at the knees. I think the problem was when the techs took them off they used an electric file thing, but honestly think he went to the deepest layer next to my skin!

SJP's Mole

I had gels once in my life and never again! Like that, they were like paper afterwards and just felt so sensitive that you'd cringe if they touched anything. I'm a nail-biter but mainly because they're so weak – they split in work, I can't find a nail file and I end up 'evening them out' with my teeth till they're all gone! I swear by Broadway Nails Real Life ones for special occasions.

yinyogi

I have to admit I loved my gels. I kept them short and worked a natural pink over them, they were fab. The only problem was the cost of upkeep! But like everyone else, my nails were a mess afterwards. I swear by OPI Nail Envy Nail Strengthener. After three months I had the strongest nails I've ever had. I buy it for everyone with dodgy nails and they all love it, seriously it will work!

Lilo

I have managed to get my nails to a nice length following gels months back. Took ages for the damage to grow out and I'm giving full credit to Sally Hansen for helping me through this difficult time.

REPAIRING NAILS AFTER GELS OR ACRYLICS

- Get the false nails removed properly. Don't rip them off yourself or you run the risk of damaging your real nails forever.

- Soak your poor damaged nails in moisture. Cuticle oil and nail oil are both good. Dr. Hauschka does a fantastic Neem Nail Oil Pen.

- Buff your nails gently with a special nail buffer to smooth out the worst of the damage.

- Bring them back up to a shine with the smooth side of the buffer. See? Much better already!

- Finish off with another few drops of cuticle oil and paint them with a super moisturising base coat. I can recommend Jessica Nails Restoration for repairing damage.

NAIL FILES

Now you know the *scéal* here. In general, always file your nails in one direction only, otherwise you run the risk of weakening the nail. Also, file before you remove polish, otherwise your nails will be weaker and more prone to splitting. Avoid metal nail files like the plague.

Glass files, on the other hand, are brill, and I'll tell you why. They never wear out and the friction caused by the glass seals the tip, helping to make it stronger. The one to try? Leighton Denny's Crystal Nail File – you can buy a set of two, so keep one at home and one in the handbag.

MAMMY SAYS

I get a pack of 10 brown emery files from the chemist down the town and they last forever. I've a few down the end of my good handbag that have been there for years and they still do the job, I'm telling you. Granted, they're a bit bald and one seems to have some kind of biscuit smushed into it, but sure, it's grand. Maybe I'll get a new pack though the next time I'm in with Dymphna collecting my prescription …

Townygirl

I have a Barbara Daly at Tesco nail block – it's quite old but it's marvellous. One side files, the next lightly sands, the next removes the slough and the last side shines. I really like it … but then, I don't do my nails all that often!

Fletch

I prefer the cushioned files like the Miss Manicure one, but I have the cardboardy ones in handbags and purses for emergencies! If one of my nails breaks, it's really sharp and can do serious damage to clothes and face, so best to have a spare file just in case!

SJP's Mole

I have the Barbara Daly at Tesco glass one. Lasts forever. Will never go back to cardboard now. I'm a chronic nail biter, one of those wans that destroy their nails if they don't have a nail file available at all times, so it's great to have one that doesn't really wear out.

Shin

A teabag, you say? My nails are hopeless. It's my own fault. When I type I use the sides of my thumb to hit the space bar – which I suppose is whacking my nail every time. Then they break about a third of the way down and it's a disaster trying to stop it snagging until it grows enough to cut it into a weird shape. Maybe I should just wear thimbles or elastic bands for typing?

Lynnie

You can't really see the teabag unless you've just used clear varnish over it and are looking very, very closely. If you use a nice coloured-y varnish, you can't see it at all at all!

TEABAG TO THE RESCUE

If you've split a nail and it's going to ruin a perfect 10, you should try this. Peel a thin strip from a teabag and glue it to your nail with superglue. Perfect for emergencies.

WORK OF SATAN:
Formaldehyde Nail Hardeners

Let's get straight to the point here. Formaldehyde is the liquid they use to embalm dead bodies. It should have been banned from nail products years ago, but it still exists in many popular base coats and nail hardeners. Basically, you don't want to paint anything on your nails that is used to preserve lab specimens and is a regular order in the funeral home.

Bee

Back in the good old days, M&S used to have nail repair kits. These included nail glue, the teabag-type material (very fine silky stuff), a buffer to tidy up the repair job and a sheet of nail plasters. The plasters were tiny ovals of clear plastic with a sticky side so you could whack them over any break and they'd stop it from catching till you got home and glued things back together again. I still have a few plasters left and keep them in my purse all the time. They are lifesavers. I haven't seen the kit in M&S for years now.

STICK-ON NAILS

Just like Goldilocks (hypothetically – we must imagine her wearing false nails), I don't want nails too long or too short. I want them to be Just Right. And that's why sometimes you just can't beat Broadway Nails.

The true joy of stick-on nails was hammered home to me while I was rushing (late, as per usual) to an evint. I had a moment of horror when I saw my raggedy, chewed fingernails. You know the sort of thing – you take ages getting ready only to be disgraced by horrible aul' unfiled, unpolished nails. Really lets the side down.

Oh, the joy of fecking everything into your handbag. How glad I was that there was an ancient half-used pack of Broadways in there. I glued them on in the car (someone else was driving, don't worry – even I'm not that good at multitasking!). By the time I arrived at the destination, I had a perfect French manicure.

These nails look real, like your own nails – only better. And none of the horrible ravages of gel nails.

You just can't beat these yokes sometimes. I love 'em. I've heard reports of them lasting over a week on careful folk and I can usually get a couple of days out of them.

SJP's Mole

I looooove Broadway short Real Life nails. They've less of a white tip than those wans, cos I'm not really into the French manicure look. I like them short but PERFECT! Yeah, they only last a day – you may be able to get two days out of them by putting the glue on both finger and fake nail before sticking, but they're not too dear and they look really natural. I was at a wedding recently and my own mother thought they were my own nails!

Flame

I think they sound like a great idea! Less waitin' around for polish to dry and you'd never get a clumpy effect. You could do them on the bus if you were goin' out in town kind of thing!

NAIL APPLIQUÉ

Not to be confused with stick-ons, Incoco Dry Nail Appliqué is a self-adhesive wonder product that's wafer thin, yet combines base, polish and top coats. Peel off the backing paper, smooth the appliqué transfer down onto nails and buff off any excess length. Bingo – a perfect 10 in literally five minutes. No mess, no drying time and no fumes. It sounds cheesy till you try it, but put them on once, accept tons of compliments on your pristine manicure, and you'll be suckered in forever more. Oh – and did I mention you can get them for toes, too?

BUFFING NAILS THE BEAUT.IE WAY

The shine, the health and the feel of natural buffed nails without polish is fantastic. And all it takes is a little square nail buffer block and 10 minutes while I'm watching *Eastenders*. Well, you need something to cheer yourself up during *Eastenders*, god knows. Buffing your nails actually makes them stronger and helps them to grow, as it increases circulation and cuts out the risk of snagging or breaking.

Here's how it works:

1. Get out your little nail buffer block (from any chemist for a few quid). Take off your old nail polish – use an acetone-free polish remover because that's kinder to your nails. Wash your hands and rub a drop of cuticle oil into your nails.

2. File your nail tips with the roughest side of the nail block and lightly sand your whole nail with the black side of the buffer. Don't go mad here – you don't want to go deep. The aim is to smooth any imperfections and even out the nail surface.

3. Now use the white part of the buffer to bring out the natural oils in your nails – 15–20 strokes will usually do it.

4. Use the grey side to shine up your nails. This is a real wow moment! (If your nail buffer isn't the regular white, grey and black colour combo, don't worry, there will probably be instructions with it.)

5. This step is optional, as your nails will look great anyway at this stage, but if you want you can finish up with another little drop of cuticle oil. Rub it in well and seal the shine in with a nourishing base coat. I love Jessica Nails Rejuvenation or Restoration. They do take ages to dry, but they really soak into the nail and give it a real treat.

Enjoy!

By the Hokey

Think your nails are long? The longest fingernails in the world belonged to Shidhar Chillal. They were an attractive 20 feet, 2.25 inches. It took 48 years to grow them. Guess he wasn't doing much housework then.

Perfect Pedis

Getting a pedicure is perfect for shameless 'me' time. Here are three very good reasons to book yourself in for that pedi.

1. Your feet will not only look gorgeous, they'll feel fab too. Total transformation, I promise you.

2. Your piggies will be painted a gorgeous chip-proof colour and look fantastic in sandals.

3. Trained hands will basically give you a foot rub for ages, scrub away dead skin, file any yellow bits, clip your toenails and rub foot balm into your heels.

minxinparis

Admiring my twinkly toes as I type, I had my spring pedi last Saturday. Recently ran a marathon, so this is my post-run treat. And boy, do the feet need it! Every night I rub Palmer's cocoa butter gunge into them (the stuff in the tub) and stick a pair of socks on top, guaranteed softness in the morning.

If you're like me, you'll never have the patience to file, pumice, scrub, rub and painstakingly paint to professional standards.

This is a fab indulgence, and if you've never had a pedicure before, indulge yourself soon. Even if it's not strictly sandal weather, it's the nicest treatment and lasts for weeks and weeks. You can hug the pleasure to yourself and love your pretty polished toes.

Top Tip: Wear flip-flops when going to get your pedicure done. Sounds obvious, but people often forget and ruin the nail polish.

MAMMY SAYS

Oh no, I wouldn't be going for pedicures and the like. There's an easier way to do it – using a few things you've lying round the house already.

I'll tell you a story. Last year I was in bed reading the new *Ireland's Own* when I happened to see Daddy's feet for the first time in years. Mary mother of god! The next day I'd to prise the wellies offa him and get to work. It's not easy to cut through those toenails – but like I always say, once you've brought up eight childer, you're not afraid of a bit of hard work. Them tough garden scissors are ideal for this kind of karehokey. Then I got out the sander and doesn't the old yella skin on his heels turn to powder and disappear quick as a flash.

PIRHANA PEDI

Fish like to clean things: each other, sharks, rocks. They nosh up all the crap that floats around the oceans and rivers and streams. It's all part of the natural cycle of nature. Fair enough.

They've been put to work busily eating up all the horrors on human feet too. All the hard skin, the scaly toes, the toe jam, the yellow heels. Delicious.

This trend, notably featured on *Ugly Betty*, originated in Turkey. You can get it done in Ireland; it's used a lot by psoriasis sufferers. Doctor fish are tiny, toothless little specimens who love to eat the most horrible, crusty, yucky skin imaginable. Feet (or your whole body if you're feeling brave) are immersed in a shallow tub of water and little fishies swim up to nibble 'em smooth. I suppose if you've got hooves they'll bring out Jaws or something.

Look, don't knock it. If they like dead skin, who are we to argue? Now if only we could teach them to put on nail varnish, we'd be sorted.

FOOT CREAM AND EXFOLIATOR

Feet get dryer than the Sahara and cracks and fissures deeper than a waterless riverbed are unfortunately all too common – unless you use a good foot cream and scrub. Enough of the foot geography though, let's get down to the recommendations.

All sorts of instant pedicure products can be found in the shops. There are also special, heavier-duty products used in salons to literally dissolve away hard, dead skin. Use one of them or any oil-rich scrub to take off all the horrible cheese rind, then lavish your feet with a special foot cream.

Deni-o

Walnut oil with sea salt is a great exfoliator. I used to use olive oil, but walnut oil is better. Makes your skin so soft and gets rid of all the yucky skin on your feet! I have spent fortunes on exfoliators and my good mum recommended that and I haven't looked back since! Also, with the money you save on such a cheap treatment, you can get yourself to Dundrum and treat yourself!

Andie

After soaking and scrubbing, try lashing on some Silcocks Base and cover with socks for overnight treatment. It's available in most chemists and very cheap, but brilliant! I've used it on my hands too – great results!

MontyC

I use Benefit's Sandal cream … and it's fantastic stuff. Comes with the cutest pair of ankle socks too!

Great Picks for Feet

 ## AISLING'S PICK

I love Vichy's Podexine range. There's a Callus Corrector and a Cracked Heel Repair cream available, which tackle even the grossest of built-up skin and sore, peeling heels. Brilliant!

Danne Montague King Calerase Exfoliant Foot Cream

You might have to do a bit of hunting high and low for this, but Danne Montague King's Calerase Exfoliant Foot Cream is brilliant for horny hooves. While it's expensive, it's used by the pros to melt away calluses and hard skin, and it works really well.

Flexitol Heel Balm

Without a doubt, it has to be Flexitol Heel Balm. Packaging that looks like it was designed using clip art notwithstanding, this stuff is fantastic for a pharmacy buy. Use it for a couple of days and you'll really notice the change.

DIY: At-home Pedicure

- Get the pedicure tub ready (a washing-up bowl is ideal) and add some bath salts, or for a bit of pampering, some scented oil.

- Remove any nail polish.

- Trim your nails straight across and file, being careful not to cut them too short.

- Soak your feet in warm water for 5–10 minutes.

- Take one foot out at a time and wipe around the nails with a clean, dry clean towel.

- Add a cuticle eliminator and give your feet a gander. Do they need callus eliminator? Do that at this point if they're looking a bit horny.

- Push back cuticles with a pedi-stick and file the excess nail exposed from soaking. Gently clean dirt from under the nails.

- File the heels of feet with pumice or use a scrub if you prefer.

- Put foot back in water, take out your other foot and repeat the steps.

- After both feet are soaked to perfection, using a foot balm or moisturiser, do a 5–10 minute massage on each foot.

- Wipe toes with polish remover to take away any oily residue, and then apply base coat, following up with your favourite nail polish.

Shivers

I tried the Scholl Nail Brightening stuff last week, but I only had time to use it on my two big toes … Well, I was out over the weekend, standing in a nightclub on Friday night, when I looked down and noticed that my big toes were glowing under the UV light! I was actually so beyond mortified that I just laughed. One of the lads noticed and kept staring before he finally asked, 'Eh, what's up with your toes … just your big toes?' I stayed brazen and told him it was a party trick! *CRINGE* First thing Saturday morning, fixed the rest of my toes! If I'm gonna glow, I may as well glow completely!

6

Water
Baby

Bathing is one of the greatest pleasures known to humankind...

BATHING BEAUT.IES

Bathing is one of the greatest pleasures known to humankind. Immersing yerself in hot steaming water really does soothe those aches and pains and is a great way to relax. And of course, bathing can be used to serve another purpose – getting ready for a Big Night Out.

WORKING BATH VS. PAMPER BATH

There are two types of baths. Both serve very specific purposes, both are indispensable.

WORKING BATH

A working bath is a short burst of maintenance and is an incredibly efficient way to get ready for a night out. I have not yet trademarked the term – but it's mine. Paris Hilton can keep 'that's hot'.

Now you can call this a booty call bath – if that's what you're after – but if you need to get ready quickly for a big night out (or a big night in), this is the one for you. If you're hoping for the latter, don't forget to wear your lucky knickers!

1. Run the bath with an uplifting and invigorating bath oil. I know bubbles are lovely, but god do they dry out the skin. Why? Cos they're generally packed full of foaming agents, which have a scaly-skin effect. You can even just add a couple of drops of essential oil to your bath – try a citrus oil. This bath will wake you up, so avoid anything with lavender, which is far better suited to relaxation.

2.	While the bath is running, cleanse and slap on a good face mask. If you're of an oily persuasion, use one that will soothe skin and soak up any sebum. Clay masks are great for this. Dry and regular skin types will love a mask that's hydrating and soothing. Plus, here's something handy: make-up will go on much more smoothly afterwards.

3.	Start scrubbing once in the bath, especially those hooves. Get rid of all that dead yucky skin with a hard loofah or a pumice stone, and if you need to shave your legs (or any other bits of you) get that done and dusted.

4.	You should have all your jobs done in 10 minutes. Out you get and smother yourself in a good body lotion or gradual tan, whichever you prefer. Wash off the face mask and you're good to go.

You should be pretty much gorgeous and glowing and ready for anything! Well, hopefully, sez you.

Great Masks for Bathtime
Clinique Deep Cleansing Emergency Mask

Clinique Deep Cleansing Emergency Mask is nice and soothing and leaves skin feeling smoother – ideal for make-up application afterwards.

Dermalogica Skin Hydrating Masque

Good old Dermalogica Skin Hydrating Masque is the business. A clear, non-scented gel, it works wonders on stroppy skin. And here's a little tip: it's great for guys too.

Top Tip: If you're running really short of time, skip the face mask. Instead, try putting on your make-up before the bath. In theory, the steam sets it, making it last longer and look fresher than usual.

Princess Lisa

Love the Sanctuary bath oil – I throw it in with the creamy bath stuff as well so I'll have bubbles too! Then for when I'm feeling swish, I love the Laura Mercier Crème Brulée or French Vanilla honey bath … absolutely heaven!

Lorna

I love Yankee Candles. Tahitian Flower, Wedding Day and Clean Cotton are my faves. Got my mam a gorgeous Jo Malone candle and she won't light it, it's for display.

girlfriday

Love the Jo Malone grapefruit candle. Also Diptyque do a gorgeous rose-scented one. L'Occitane has a great selection as well, and the Cloon Keen vanilla one with the ice cream cone on it is gorge.

PAMPER BATH

Now this is the one we all know and love. A pamper bath is for serious Me Time.

There are steps to take, but sure, that would just make the whole thing too formal, and what we want is to induce a state of relaxed bliss.

So no steps here, just suggestions. Run the bath, nice and deep. Fill it with a generous amount of a gorgeous bath oil. Sanctuary Bath Relaxer is fantastic, but if you're really splashing out (see what I did there?), try Jo Malone's beautiful bath oils.

Light your scented candles. If you've never tried the whole candle vibe before, trust me, it adds so much.

Treat your hair with a good dollop of an intensive treatment like James Brown London Moisture Mask for Hair and wrap in clingfilm. Put on your face mask. The steam and warmth will help both masks to penetrate deeply and work more efficiently.

Pour your glass of wine.

Now there's nothing left to do but wallow like a mini hippo, using your big toe to top up the hot water.

WHY POSH-SCENTED CANDLES?

Expensive scented candles are expensive for a couple of good reasons. First, they last for ages. Their burn time in hours is usually really impressive because they use high-quality waxes. Make sure you trim the wick regularly, though – I know it's hard to talk of wicks and the trimming of them with a straight face, but here we are. An untrimmed wick means that the candle can burn up to twice as fast.

Cheapie smelly candles are sometimes only sprayed with scent on the outside. Expensive ones are choc full of gorgeous scented ingredients and essential oils – meaning that they smell delicious, last for a longer time and can really calm and relax.

Plus there's something totally decadent and luxurious about lighting a fabulous Jo Malone or Diptyque candle – just for you, just for your Me Time. Marks & Spencer also do gorgeous scented candles and are a great cheaper alternative to the luxe brands.

And don't forget the great candles that are made right here on our fair shores, ladies. We love the scented creations from Cloon Keen, Max Benjamin and the treatment candle range from Nádúr Organics. Scrummy.

Gio

I love Molton Brown candles. They last for ages and their packaging is gorgeous so you can re-use the boxes they come in!

Polly

I have the Max Benjamin Lemongrass and Ginger candle and I love it! Muji do a gorgeous cinnamon and mandarin one for about €7. It's in a tin so it's great for travelling. Good for getting rid of that 'hotel room smell'! I love L'Occitane candles but I usually buy the oil version instead if it's available, as they are more economical.

DIY: Take a Tea Bath

Go on, go on, go on, go on, go on.

Ah go on. What's not to like? Tea is soothing and relaxing, so imagine how a whole bath full of aromatic, steaming ingredients can dissolve stress. Light a smelly candle, lie back, close your eyes, make sure you can reach the hot water tap with your toes to top up the heat and put a Do Not Disturb sign on the door.

Now, what to put in it? Not a Lyons pyramid teabag. You can buy sachets of bath tea-type mixtures, of course, but why not use this as an opportunity to go all DIY?

Get an old pair of tights (make sure they've gone through the wash, though, otherwise you'll get a whole different bathing experience). Stuff a section with herbs and tie up the top.

You can use just about any dried herbs or flowers you like – here are some suggestions:

- Dried lavender for relaxation.
- Dried thyme to soothe.
- Bath salts and cider vinegar for detox.
- A mix of camomile, peppermint and green teas.
- Dried lemon or orange rind.
- Add a few drops of any essential oil you like to the bathwater.

Put the 'tea bag' in the bath and run the water. Let it steep for a few minutes and swirl it around to release the ingredients.

Complete the experience with a DIY salt scrub – mix sea salt and olive oil for a natural (and cheap) exfoliation (see p. 94).

TEDDY BOBBS ADVISES

Even the dogs on the street know that running a bath is pure expense. A shower uses up far less hot water. Sure, you'd be having the immersion on for ages for a bath – over a year that adds up to a substantial amount, I'm telling ye. All money you could be lashing away into a regular saver account at 4 per cent.

Well, at least I can stop you from filling the bath full of expensive oils and bubbles. Try this concoction here, it's good and cheap.

Mix a mug of pure sea salt* with $\frac{1}{2}$ teaspoon of liquid glycerin. Mix in a few drops of a scented oil if you're hell bent on getting it smelling nice (in my opinion it's not necessary, but I'll let it go). Sprinkle the mixture into a hot bath and wallow, knowing you're having a lovely bath that's saving a few cents.

* Make sure to use sea salt here. Ordinary table salt has had all the minerals removed and won't give you any health or well-being benefits, and can also be dangerous for people with high blood pressure.

SHOWER GELS AND WASHES

This is something that we all use a lot of – or Jesus, we should anyway. Most of us get through gallons of this stuff over the year, so consequentially we all tend to know a lot about it.

When Tish left a comment to say 'Whatever's on special in Tesco, Boots or Penneys does me', it rang bells with a lot of us. I mean, shower gel or soap is something that you just use to wash yourself, and once it smells okay and does the job, that's fine.

But if you really want a treat, what are the best of the genre at all, at all? The genre of pampering showering lotions/potion/gels, that is.

Liz

I LOVE, LOVE, LOVE this scent. Got the shower gel, the body moisturiser and the shimmery perfume as a gift, thanks to my lubely husbag.

Em

I'm alternating between the Heavenly Gingerlily shower gel and Bliss Lemon and Sage Soapy Sap at the moment, both smell sooo gorgeous. Love the Heavenly Gingerlily body lotion too and the slight shimmer you get with it. Always have a Molton Brown shower gel on the go since I started using it about 18 months ago. I would get red, dry patches on my skin, especially the tops of my arms, when I came out of the shower, but this stopped when I switched to Molton Brown. Blissful Templetree is my favourite and the matching body lotion is perfect for summer, very light and cooling.

Shower Gel Splurge

Molton Brown is truly a range apart and the Heavenly Gingerlily Moisture Bath & Shower gel is as fabilis as they come. It's delicately scented and a rich brown colour in the bottle. As soon as the heat of the water hits it, the fragrance develops and intensifies. Exotic (the ingredients are sourced in Tahiti) and aromatically moisturising, this is deservedly one of the brand's best-sellers.

GREEN AND GORGEOUS

While they're not strictly speaking organic, we do love Organic Surge's lovely shower gels. Packed full of essential oils and with nothing that'll dry delicate skin out, they're a good price and a portion of profits go to African children's charities too.

Imperial Leather Skinbliss

This entire range is lovely and you can pick it up at the supermarket.

SMELL YOU LATER!

Bliss Lemon + Sage Soapy Sap is so delicious that you really can't be held responsible for your actions.

I bought Kirstie a bottle of this for her birthday. I'd gotten her her proper present anyway, so this was just a little extra. It arrived. Oh goodie! I put it in a bag, ready to give to her – and promptly forgot all about it. Till the weekend after the birthday …

I spotted it on Saturday morning while still in my pyjamas and waking up over a mug of coffee. I had a sniff. OMG – I had forgotten just how gorgeous this stuff is. Sage and lemon smells fresh and zingy. Addictive. I couldn't resist the lure of the Soapy Sap. I hurried upstairs to have a shower. Divine! Then The Husband started sniffing the air, remarking on the scent in the bathroom. So he had to have a go of it too.

Sorry Kirstie, I shouldn't have used your present for myself, but I couldn't help it. And I've ordered you a new one – who knows, you might even get given it this time …

AISLING'S PICK:

Know the one that's one too many. Aaaah, I wish I did. Well, I usually do (honest), but sure, you know yourself, one drink leads to another and it's all fun and laughing and a bit of slagging thrown in and the wine keeps flowing…

Harto

Girls, if you tried the La Roche-Posay you wouldn't be able to go back to supermarket brands! It leaves skin just so soft and smooth! No need for moisturiser, so well worth the price.

Ellie

For me it has to be a Korres shower gel. They are DIVINE! You need the tiniest amount, the fragrances are lovely (my fave has to be the jasmine one) and they leave your skin smooth, hydrated and comfortable. I always use a body lotion anyway, force of habit, but with these shower gels I don't feel as though my skin needs one as they are so gentle.

Thing

The Nivea Happy Time shower cream is gorgeous and bargainific ... really orangey and perfect for summer (and the Boy uses the new blokey Nivea one which is good too.) The best shower gel though is either Clarins Eau Dynamisante shower mousse or L'Occitane Amande Shower Oil ... although I always feel a bit off paying that much for something that goes down the plughole!

We were out with friends having the most gorgeous dinner. It had taken us three weeks to get a table in this particular restaurant, so we sure as hell were going to make the most of it while we were there.

Anyway, the next morning I woke up in need of a big glass of juice. My skin was dehydrated too. I turned to La Roche-Posay Lipikar Surgras to deal with this situation. This stuff is truly gorgeous. It's a shower cream that smells like roses and has a rich, luxurious texture. After the shower, my skin was silky soft and nourished – with no effort required by lazy me at all. Just what I like!

This is a product that works. It's a real treat for your skin. Get some, you'll absolutely love it.

Best of the Rest

Also big faves of mine are Body Shop shower gels and L'Occitane. Mmm mmm mmm.

I'm unfairly leaving men out of the whole luxury shower recommendation because it's been my experience that they couldn't care less what they scrub up with. Once it smells kind of manly, it's fine. As the husband says, 'Sure, it's only for the aul' *liathróids* anyway.' A case of Too Much Information? I think so.

Yeh Wha? The Origins of 'Chartrey'

When I originally wrote about Nivea Bath Care Pampering Shower Oil I had one big concern: it's very runny and I felt an awful lot of it ended up not on me but on the chartrey and thus to the plughole.

This, of course, necessitated explanation. You know yer man Duncan Stewart of *About the House* fame? He's got a weird way of pronouncing some words. We tried to figure out for *ages* what the hell this 'chartrey' he was always on about was. We finally realised it was a shower tray.

A subject of massive hilarity to teenage Aisling and Kirstie, now the shower tray is forevermore known as a chartrey.

Dewy
I love Tesco Finest almond shower gel (and its scrub and body butter) and The Body Shop White Musk shower gel.

GREEN AND GORGEOUS

We're quite simply spoiled in Ireland with the amount of natural treats for bath and shower time. Situated on the very edge of Europe with thousands of miles of Atlantic between us and the nearest land mass, is it any wonder that we have so many natural and sea-based treats?

With superb brands like Voya, Nádúr and Seavite, there's loads of choice. Here's my top earth-friendly pick.

Voya Squeaky Clean

One of the best things about Beaut.ie is the fantastic goodies we get to try. All the new stuff, the latest, the greatest. Sometimes the not so great too – but what can I say except we suffer for our art sometimes.

I can't wax lyrical enough about Voya, though. This is a fantastic range. Organic, natural, cruelty free, using only top-notch ingredients, it's made by the owners of the Strandhill seaweed baths.

So it's no surprise to learn that this range is seaweed-based and therefore natural, pure and detoxifying. The first product I tried was the Squeaky Clean body wash – so fab. If I had to compare it to another shower gel I would say Bliss Soapy Sap, which I love, but this is sharper, zestier, zingier.

CELEB BEAUTY SECRETS: Cleopatra

This has to be the worst-kept beauty secret ever. To keep her skin soft and smooth, Cleopatra bathed in asses' milk. I know a good few asses, but I'm not sure if they've got any milk suitable for bathing in.

Thankfully, bathing technology has moved on in the last two thousand-odd years, but if you still fancy the Cleopatra bath, spas do a very nice version of it indeed (enjoyed by me on a few occasions). Or at home, try tipping condensed milk into your bath to get … an effect. I'm not saying what the effect will be, though. My advice? Go with a nice bath oil.

SEAWEED BATHING

The seaweed baths on the west coast of Ireland are famous, and rightly so. They get rave reviews over and over again on Beaut.ie.

Famous for their health-giving, detoxing and beautifying properties, seaweed baths have been popular for a long, long time. Oh, and your skin will be smooth as a baby's bum after one, too!

One of our regular commenters, Gio, visited one of the famed Sligo seaweed baths and told us: 'The seaweed bath is lovely, the water is just deliciously warm and not at all gloopy. The water is an amber colour and this is caused by the extraction of iodine from the seaweed and Atlantic water. One of nature's richest sources of this therapeutic element, it's fantastically moisturising for the skin (a seaweed bath has the consistency of olive oil!) and so good for you; it's completely natural, nothing added, nothing taken away.'

BOOZY FLOOZY

Well it's not the most glamorous thing in the whole world, but it feels really healthy and calming. You get a room with a steam/shower thingy and also a bath which is full of the seaweed, harvested every day nearby. The water is seawater pumped in and heated up. Then they tell you to alternate between

Cacamilis
I went for a steam seaweed bath and I have to say it was gorgeous. The steam bath was a clunky contraption that smelled brilliant – hopefully there were no hidden cameras showing me sitting in a wood box with my red face sticking out! The seaweed bath was great – really warm, clean and 'greasy' – I mean 'greasy' in a good way. After simmering for about half an hour, slurping some oxegenated water and sweating all my impurities away, I felt great. The seaweed is brought down from Donegal, is changed after every client and then the dishy doctor uses it for compost in his vegetable garden. Highly recommended.

Principessa
I got a packet of dried seaweed and I had absolutely gorgeous skin afterwards. You get a second bath out of it too. Granted, the bathroom stank like Dollymount for a bit after, but the softness of my skin made it worth suffering.

the steam room and the bath to encourage the seaweed to work at moisturising your skin and hair. You should let your head go right back because it really feels lovely in your hair – the seawater and the heat bring out the seaweed's oils. They also tell you to keep drinking water to avoid dehydration and you can share a room with a pal and keep swapping from bath to shower. Really enjoyed it and skin felt lovely afterwards.

DIY: Nádúr Organics Detox Bath Box

If you want to try out a seaweed bath at home, this is the product I recommend. Their slogan advises us to 'be pure, be natural and be gorgeous', and the quality of the products and the ingredients sure live up to this promise.

First things first: the packaging is gorgeous. In fact, it's so nice I didn't want to open the pretty little ribbon and actually use the contents. But in the end, tired and cranky after a day in which nothing had gone my way and after I'd ended up eating a huge slice of chocolate cake in the Avoca Café, I could resist the lure of the Detox Box no longer.

I ran a hot bath, lit the organic candle and put the seaweed sachet in the water to soak. After 10 minutes it releases a gel and it's time for you to rub the sachet into your skin to get the full benefit of the detoxifying nutrients. You then add up to 10 drops of the delicious-smelling essential oil blend to the bathwater. Then … relax! You're surrounded by delicious fragrances steaming up from the water and filling the air from the candle.

FLOATATION TANKS

When I heard that an hour in a float tank is equal to eight hours of deep sleep, I had to try it. Even though I wasn't sure that I would like the experience, I thought nothing ventured, nothing gained. Here's how I got on.

On the way to have my first float, the following things happened.

11:45 a.m. Upon setting the house alarm to leave the house, juggling keys, bag and other items, Cosmo Cat selected the very last split millisecond of time to zip through the closing front door, thus setting off the alarm (and not for the first time displaying an intuitive knowledge of physics and a genius-level spatial ability). Cosmo Cat was ejected from the house (after causing as much disruption and time wasting as possible by running up the stairs and hiding under the bed/ spare bed/high up in a wardrobe). Result: Much searching and cursing and eventual location and inevitable escape.

11:51 a.m. Cosmo Cat managed to repeat this whole process twice more.

12:00 p.m. Finally backed out of the drive, heartily hating Cosmo Cat.

12:32 p.m. Navigated serious roadworks and an encounter with a White Van Man which left my nerves in shreds. Desperately late for appointment.

1:34 p.m. Finally arrived. Felt like I needed a large brandy and was tempted to nip into the nearest pub, but restrained myself. Apologised insanely for lateness.

The water is warm and completely buoyant. A huge amount of salt holds you up in the water. No part of your body touches the floor of the tank. It's an incredible feeling and like nothing I've ever experienced before. Yes, you are actually floating. It's like being back in the womb, it's warm and dimly lit and comforting, and soft classical music plays.

Principessa
I think it is the most divine way to spend an hour or what seems like eight. To borrow a phrase, 'what the world needs now is a float, sweet float' – world peace would be upon us in no time! My own personal tank is a lotto win fantasy.

At first I thought I'd be bored in there for a whole hour. I started to think about popping into the supermarket on the way home and the chemist to pick up a prescription, ringing the bank and …

The lid was lifting! My god! An hour had passed – I must have fallen asleep. This has *never* happened to me before. I'm a chronic insomniac and find sleep almost impossible.

If you want to do one thing today that will reduce your stress levels and chill you out like never before, then go for a float. Just one word of caution: don't do what I did and epilate your legs the morning of your float, as salt water + freshly epilated legs = sting!

SPA BATHING

I have to say this is a spa treatment I adore and I've had many of these baths. They come in all sorts of flavours: wine, chocolate, milk – pick your favourite.

In fact, any time I'm in a spa I will usually plump for one of these baths as part of the whole experience. One of the best, most enjoyable treatments I've ever had was a Cleopatra Bath finished off with a sparkling gold body treatment at the Inchydoney Spa in Cork.

The first spa bath I ever took was a wine bath. Wine is well known for its antioxidant properties, is great for the skin and for promoting a feeling of well-being throughout the body. I have to admit that I'd gotten that feeling of well-being the night before from downing a few glasses of vino, and now I was feeling the after-effects. So this was hair of the dog – but a very different one than the normal. I can't do hair of the dog anyway. Ugh. All I'm fit for is a rasher sandwich and a mug of tea.

This bath was the colour of white wine – Viña Sol, let us say. And it smelled of grapes. The water boiled with energy. Like a Jacuzzi on speed or similar drug, it bubbled violently. It spat, it gushed, and I held on for dear life. But then I got used to it and relaxed into it.

Underwater jets pummelled my muscles, moving from my back to my shoulders, up and down my legs and – my favourite bit – feet.

I got out of the bath, my whole body tingling and totally refreshed. And so began a beaurriful friendship.

7

Gorillas in the Mist

Reading the waxing menu in a particularly fancy salon can be like deciphering a foreign language or the menu at Starbucks...

SHAVING

Every gal knows that the quickest and easiest way to get rid of any fur is to shave it off. Simple. But of course for every pro in the world of beauty, there is an equal and opposite con. Shaving takes regular discipline. If you don't want to see a five o'clock shadow appearing on your legs, you've got to know how quickly (and darkly) your hair grows back and act accordingly. You must also use the proper tools. It's no use using that orange disposable razor that's been in the bathroom cabinet since last summer (i.e. the last time you shaved your legs) and hoping for the best. Legs cut to ribbons, a fetching red rash and hairy patches will only be the half of it.

Leg shaving has only really become popular since World War II. Stockings were few and far between and women resorted to shaving their legs so they could then dye them with gravy or tea and draw a black line down the back. Yummy!

You have to admire the ingenuity they showed, but you can also feel free to curse the trend they started for hair-free legs.

Yes, I know you've been shaving your legs for years – maybe not since WW2 – but there is an actual proper way to do it. And let's face it, nothing beats shaving for silky smooth pins. So unless you want legs cut to ribbons (and missed bits), here's how to go about it.

- Lather up. The easiest way to cut your legs to bits is to shave dry skin.
- Shaving oil is great, but I prefer foam. Why? Cutting a great big swathe through the foam is a satisfying way of ensuring you've accessed all areas. Unlike a friend of mine who, glancing down at her freshly shaved legs one sunny day at a barbeque, noticed that she'd left an unflattering hairy ankle bracelet on each leg.

- Exfoliate before you shave. This raises the hairs and leaves the ground prepared, as it were.

- Pick a nice sharp razor and change the blades regularly. A blunt one will do you no favours. See the top tip on men's razors below.

- Those cheap aul' disposable things are crapola – avoid them unless you like pain and blood.

- If you run out of foam or oil, use hair conditioner. It's only brilliant.

- Shave upwards from your ankle, against the way hair grows, towards your knee.

- Lash on the moisturiser afterwards and you're done. Don't forget to check for the hairy bracelet!

MEN'S RAZORS

- Men's razors rock. Anyone who's ever shaved their legs with one knows these things are the business. Why do you think he goes so mad when you nick his Mach Fusion Power Hundred Blade contraption? He knows something you don't – and he doesn't want you blunting it with leg stubble.

- Manly shaving foam is just as good for shaving your legs – it's just not pink and doesn't smell of sweets. And it's cheaper.

- If you must have a girly razor, go for one of the Gillette Venus family – they're the best. And remember that the heads are interchangeable – for instance, even if you originally bought a Breeze, you can still click a Divine head on top.

Lynnie

Totally agree about boy razors, they are the shizz! And I bought Himself his Gillette Fusion Power and his last lot of blades so it's OK for me to sneakily use it, right?

Kirstie

Men's razors are amazing, it's so true. I am still adoring my Venus Breeze though, which is hands-down the best women's shaver out there.

trilby

I find this tip really helps to avoid those horrible 'shaving bumps'. Always shave in an upwards direction (i.e. from the ankle to knee) to remove hair – and then go back over the same strip of skin in a downwards direction. Not sure how it works, but it definitely makes skin less bumpy.

Waxing

If you actually stop to think about it, waxing is one of the more bizarre beauty rituals we have. Consider it in all its barbaric glory. You pay to go and lie down in a room and get hot wax smeared all over your legs. Then the wax is ripped off by a lady in a white *guna*. And make no mistake about it – no matter how it's described in the brochures, it's gonna hurt.

Women rush from the office in their lunch hour to get a bikini wax, swap news at coffee breaks about the best places to get it done and certainly wouldn't dream of jetting off aboard a Ryanair flight to the sun without getting a waxing fix. Waxing is the bread and butter work of many a beauty salon.

Guide to Bikini Waxes

fabatforty

I had a bikini wax recently and I suspect the girl was newish and got a bit bored halfway through (I am a hairy Mary!). It's a bit embarrassing when the therapist asks you if you think that's enough waxing done or will she keep going. Eh yeah, that why I'm here!

Reading the waxing menu in a particularly fancy salon can be like deciphering a foreign language or the menu at Starbucks. All you want is a regular coffee, but you're forced to ask for a double mocha latte frappe cappuccino grande so as not to look like an unsophisticated fool.

There's absolutely nothing wrong with saying 'I'd just like to tidy things up so I look decent in my new high-legged swimsuit' or 'I want the whole lot off.' You don't have to know that the first one is a high bikini and the second is an extreme Hollywood.

Remember that the fashion for Brazilians is nothing more than a fashion. Feel free to buck the trend and stay au naturel, just tidying up any spiders' legs that may peek out of your bikini bottoms. Remember Miranda in the *Sex and the City* movie? None of us wants to see that, surely.

- Hollywood: All off. Check your modesty in with your coat in reception.
- Brazilian: Thin line left in the centre. Bum and undercarriage waxed.
- High bikini: Great for high-legged bikinis or knickers. Basically a Brazilian without the 'underneath bit'.
- Bikini: Just enough to ensure no spiders' legs are poking out of your knickers. Recommended for the modest.
- Variations: Salons might offer different colours, shapes or crystal enhancements and call them all different names. If you're feeling adventurous, go for it.

What Happens During a Brazilian?

When waxing virgin Angel asked one day what actually happens during a Brazilian wax, she was deluged with replies. I picked Clarence's comment because it's very descriptive and leaves nothing to the imagination. If you have a delicate constitution, you can skip this bit.

Angel
I have a very important question. I am a Brazilian waxing virgin and I really want to get it done. Actually, I want a Hollywood (that's the whole lot off, isn't it?!). What I really really want to know is what *exactly* does it involve? How long does it take, how embarrassing is it and how bad is the pain? Can anyone please give me honest answers?

Clarence

Angel – it's like a bad plaster ripping off sensation at worst but obviously that will depend on your pain threshold generally. Take a Nurofen or two about half an hour beforehand if you have concerns on that front. Embarrassment factor is up to you – these girls have seen it all before and it doesn't cost them a thought. You will be naked from waist down, legs pulled up to your chin/middle for the wax to be done on the bum area, then same pose as if ordinary bikini wax. But the regrowth can be itchy and annoying – I would start with a Brazilian and see how you feel about it before embarking on a Hollywood. Best thing I ever did though – couldn't be without waxing now.

Kirstie

A friend recently recounted a tale of woe at the beauty salon. In she'd gone for a wax job on her nethers, as they needed a tidying, and she'd requested a Brazilian. But what she got was the sort of Brazilian you'd expect Sister Concepta from school to give you. Less landing strip and more landing field, she deemed the result 'the Catholic Brazilian'.

Lynnie

Re: the pain aspect – the number one thing is to be careful of the time of the month you get your waxing done. Coming up to and shortly after your period, the pain will be much worse and will absolutely lift you out of it. If you can afford it and depending on your own rate of regrowth, getting your waxing done every three to four weeks will help lessen the pain as the root of the hair won't be as strong as it would be if you were to leave six weeks between sessions.

Mel

Before my wedding I thought I'd brave it and go for my first ever Brazilian (it only took a few years of extended waxing to get the nerve up). She dropped a huge glob of wax right, ahem, in the centre shall we say – where the little landing strip should have been. I looked at her red face with fear. And that is how I had my first Hollywood. Except she wasn't fully trained for that wax and I was left with a weird ring of hair on the underside and NO landing strip. I ended up shaving the remaining 'ring' that night (big mistake, as it itched the entire honeymoon as it grew back!).

DOUBLE DIPPING

Things can get very intimate during a wax, that's for sure, so you put your trust in the salon that it will be doing everything it can to make sure hygiene and cleanliness are of the highest standard. Right? Well, unfortunately in a lot of cases you'd be wrong. Unlike in the US or the UK, for example, where much stricter standards are adhered to, Irish salons are not regulated in the same way. This means the practice of double dipping is widespread.

Wax pots are only heated to 40 degrees – any hotter and they'd burn the skin – but this is not hot enough to kill bacteria. The wooden spatulas that spread the wax are disposable. They should be binned every time they touch the skin and a new one used to dip into the pot. Otherwise, skin cells and other bacteria will be passed back into the waxing pot. Multiply this practice by numerous clients all using the same waxing pot for their intimate treatments, and you've got something incredibly unhygienic.

Yet this is standard practice in most Irish salons. Watch out for it the next time you go in and ask the salon why they don't use small individual pots of wax – there are loads of disposable or one-use products out there for them to use. I'll hazard a guess: could it be because it's less hassle for them to use the big communal pot of wax and no one is making them do otherwise? It's nasty and unhygienic and the sooner a stop is put to it, the better.

Beckie

I'm a therapist and I work in a salon that uses an individual wax system. There are a few I know of. Ask your salon if they use any of these: Phd waxing, Australian system or the egg wax system. They have applicators that are thrown in the bin after use – no pot to double dip in!

Great Picks for Waxing at Home

Let's not pretend: home wax isn't nearly as effective as a salon service, but if you urgently need to get rid of a Ronnie or a few spiders' legs, then fear not, there are products out there that will do a reasonable job for you.

Cold Wax

Cold wax strips are a really common choice for home waxing because they're relatively fuss-free and easy to use. Pick up a set of strips in any chemist and remember that practise makes perfect! I reckon Veet makes the best of the (not hugely effective) bunch.

Red Mum
I do a little home waxing using Smooth Appeal. There is a stovetop version, but I think the microwave version is even better, less painful. However, you do need to include a cup of water in with the wax to melt it, as the last time I used it, I blew up the microwave.

Hot Wax

Hot wax can be messy but tends to be more effective because the liquid wax grips the hair better. There are cooker-top and microwave options out there and I plump for the microwave versions, as they're just that bit quicker. Smooth Appeal is the one to try.

Top Tip: Gooey bits left over that you know your tights will instantly stick to? Lash a bit of baby oil on a cotton pad and watch that leftover wax disappear instantly.

Guys and Hair Removal

You might not be ready for a mankini just yet, but perhaps you want to look a bit smoother in the swimming pool. So remember fellas, many, many men get waxed, not just Brian O'Driscoll. It's far more common than you'd think. Whether it's back, shoulders, chest or eyebrows, the therapist will be well used to getting you smooth and confident again. For a back, sack and crack wax, though, you might need to check out a specialist, as not every therapist is trained to do this.

Back Hair

A lot of men regularly resort to using hair removal cream to get rid of back and shoulder hair. Hair removal cream is, to put it bluntly, a pain in the ass, so if you can dispense with that messy, stinky option, do. Plus you probably have to get your wife or girlfriend to do it for you.

Laser, or intense pulse light (IPL), hair removal is a very popular option with men. It's well worth the discomfort of a course of IPL if it gets rid of the back hair that you absolutely can't stand for good.

Hot Fuss: Permanent Hair Removal

Laser hair removal is currently the hot method of permanent hair removal. (Remember electrolysis? Like the hole in the ozone layer, there was so much palaver about this at the time – now it seems to have been much ado about nothing.)

IPL is a laser system that zaps hair down in the root to kill it. It's uncomfortable, and if you're getting it done in a sensitive area, you'll have to clench your teeth. In fact, use this time to make a full and frank confession of your sins to God.

It takes a whole lot of grit and determination for permanent methods of hair removal to succeed. You have to be disciplined and make sure you stick to the schedule, or else it ain't gonna work.

Glamgirl

I was thinking of getting laser done on my legs. I got my underarms done a few years ago, and I find it brill. When you look at the amount you spend in the year on waxing, the laser treatment would pay off in eight years or less.

Kelly

I'm getting laser on the ole bikini too and it's brill. I used to get terrible ingrown hairs and couldn't wax at all. I have only had three sessions so far and it's worth every penny when you think how much you spend over the years on waxing.

I've had IPL laser treatments, but the thing is, you have to wait six weeks between treatments for the whole cycle of hair growth to begin again so the hair can be zapped effectively. IPL only works on hair that is actively growing at the time of the zap, so it takes about five or six cycles of laser for it all to be killed properly. And during that time, you can't pluck, wax or epilate, as you'd rip out the root, thus negating the whole process. The only option open to you is shaving, and when you're getting facial hair lasered, I have to be honest – it's not a good option. Suffice it to say I abandoned laser after a few goes. I totally wimped out and went back to waxing.

But I'm a bit of a lazy yoke. Laser does work – I've heard absolutely glowing reports from lots of people and I'm more than willing to step back into the breach. But – and there is a but – the hair will grow back eventually and you'll have to go for top-up treatments to be re-zapped. So when they say permanent, they mean 'a little bit permanent'.

Salon Secrets

When I heard about the bloke who was getting laser done *inside his nose* I felt myself break out in a cold sweat. He absolutely hated the hairs sprouting from his nose and wanted rid of them, no matter how much pain he went through.

EPILATING

I'll confess to having a love–hate affair with my epilator. I love that it whips hair out by the root and leaves me fur-free for weeks. I love that it's cheap and doesn't necessitate any mess or wax or foam. I love that it doesn't require booking a salon appointment.

Now I'm not going to lie to you – it does hurt. But so does waxing. If you can handle wax, you can put up with epilation.

But I absolutely hate that epilation causes so many bloody ingrown hairs. Like no other method of depilation, it will leave you with many cursed lumps and bumps. The action of the epilator can break hairs under the surface of the skin, causing them to grow back crookedly (for want of a better word) or sideways under the skin. They can't break free, so they curl themselves into an unsightly red lump, which wasn't the effect you wanted at all, now was it?

trillian

I'm a big fan of epilators – you don't have to wait for your hair to grow, like waxing, and you don't get stubble as it grows back! I've been epilating under my arms for years, and to be honest I don't really need to do it any more because the hairs have all but disappeared.

Ava

I use the Bliss pads for the first few days after a wax (after showering) and then again for a few days as soon as I notice any regrowth. They prevent the little buggers changing direction in the first place. I was never plagued with ingrown hairs, but I never get any at all now.

Melly

I really am plagued by ingrowns. My bikini line is always patchy and this really puts me off going for a wax. A bit too much info perhaps! Once it got so bad I had to go to the doctor. She called it folliculitus – inflammation of the hair follicles – and put me on antibiotics.

Anyway, when I started using the epilator I knew none of this. Innocently I epilated and was delighted with the results. No more waxing! This would save me a fortune. No more shaving! This would save loads of time. But there's no such thing as a free lunch, is there?

You've got to be much more aware with the epilator. I've tried various things, some of which worked, some of which didn't. Here's a three-step rundown of what works:

1. Exfoliate before you epilate.
2. Lash on the body lotion afterwards.
3. Use a product to prevent ingrown hairs. They do actually work. You just need to rub them over any epilated areas and they'll let the hair grow back up straight. The one I really like is Bliss Ingrown Hair Eliminating Peeling Pads. And check out your local chemist for a brilliant roller-ball number called PFB Vanish too. It doesn't look the most glamorous, but because it's packed full of salicylic acid, it's nifty at preventing ingrown lumps and bumps.

PRODUCT OF YORE: Jolen Creme Bleach

Remember those orange moustaches? Brings back memories, huh? Although this stuff has improved its formulation, the memory of fluorescent 'taches stays with me forever. Don't use this. Get yer Ronnie waxed instead.

A WORLD OF PAIN

Why the hell does it all have to hurt so much? Be it ladygarden, legs or eyebrows, hairs are ripped out of their follicles in salons and bedrooms all over the land every day in the name of beauty. Mama mia, the things we will endure – and pay to have done to us. Is there anything that will take the sting out of it?

- **Topical preparations:** These are usually creams that come in a tube. You slap the stuff onto the area about to be waxed and in 35 to 40 minutes you will be numbed sufficiently to make the pain less agonising. Try No Scream Cream, a nifty tube you can pick up in most salons that offer waxing services.
- **Painkillers:** My poison of choice. Take a couple of Paracetamol or Nurofen about half an hour before you go to get waxed and you'll find the proceedings much more bearable.
- **A stiff drink:** Or two stiff drinks. I know people who swear by it.
- **General anaesthetic:** If you're considering this, I'd advise you to stick to shaving.

Shivers

I sometimes find waxing quite painful, I have to say. Though last time I was getting my bikini line done, there were screams from another room. 'Oh, must be someone getting waxed,' announced the beautician quite calmly. My jaw dropped. Clearly there's someone who finds it worse than me.

Mini-bikini

Here's my advice: one or two shots of something strong (maybe whiskey?) and you won't care where they're rippin' hair. It will completely get rid of the embarrassment factor, and you won't care about your pocket suffering (not until the morning anyway, tee hee).

WORK OF SATAN: Hair Removal Creams

They're messy. They stink. They run the risk of burning the skin off you. Quite often they don't work. In short, avoid. A true Work of Satan

MAMMY SAYS

Crazy, yis are. Madness! Leave it grow – Daddy never seemed to mind.

DYE YOUR BETTY

You can get all manner of dyes and shapes in specialist salons. But if you want to do it at home, downstairs stencils, crystals and dyes are all available and becoming more and more popular – check out the Betty Beauty range of down-below dyes.

If you've spotted a stray grey or two, simply dye the lot and keep your youthful colour. Perhaps you're concerned that your cuffs don't match your collar? With the use of colour, not even those closest to you will know you're not a natural blonde.

And don't forget – just for laughs you can turn your cha-cha a 'fun' shade like bright pink.

LauraF

All I can think of is if you had to go into hospital and for some reason you were exposed! With a pink Betty! Remember what your mammy used to say: always wear clean knickers in case you get knocked down by a bus!

ams

My friend, a nurse, told me about a girl who came into the hosp with her, ahem, Betty dyed *green*! She was getting her appendix out or something. Anyway, after they had shaved and prepared the patient, the consultant wrote 'mowed the lawn' on her chart! She swears this is true!

LADYGARDENS OF YORE: The Merkin

If the fashion for Brazilians fades, a lot of girls could be left feeling a little draughty. So what do you if you're shorn like a sheep and all the magazines tell you you should be sporting an Afro on your cha–cha? Well, ignore them, would be the obvious advice. Or you could invest in a Merkin.

That's right – a stick-on ladygarden wig to make things look full and fluffy. Merkins have a very unsavoury origin. When they came into vogue in the eighteenth century, it was to save the blushes of syphilitic prostitutes whose hair had dropped out. Ugh. But they're still around today and you can buy them from the Internet. You'll be rushing to do that, so.

Blue Box Wax

This is known as the Tiffany (because it apparently looks like one of their jewellery boxes). It's a variation on the Brazilian theme, really. You get your downstairs waxed into a square shape, you'll be dyed powder blue and a little crystal will be stuck to the middle of the whole confection.

Dollymix
I would love the blue box! How cool would that be for my 'something blue' on the wedding day? Surprise for my new hubby that night anyway!

8

Little Miss Sunshine

WHAT ARE THE MOST COMMON TAN MISTAKES AND HOW CAN WE AVOID THEM?

EMBRACE THE FAKE

I don't want to get all heavy on your ass, but it's time to get serious.

Make no mistake – Irish folk are not able for the sun. We're too pale. Do you remember what we used to look like in the summers before high-factor suncream was invented? I'll never forget memories of Pat Spillane doing the Iron Man. He was red raw, his Kerry skin burnt the flame hue of a bottle of ketchup. Ouch. Triple ouch.

But we do love the sun, and we do love to take the tinge of blue off our skin. So the minute – no, the second – the sun shines, out we rush, divesting ourselves of as many garments as possible, big white beer bellies bared without a care in the world – and that's only the women. Ah, ya boya ya! Because we know it might be raining again in the next five minutes, no matter what Evelyn Cusack said last night on the weather.

Lying on the beach on your holliers is fine – once you're plastered in sunblock – high-factor sunblock at that. Because if you don't, you're looking at premature ageing and skin cancer. The most common kind of cancer in Ireland is skin cancer.

Getting a tan from a sunbed is downright dangerous. You'd be mad to go down this route.

Thank jaysus we're learning a bit of sense, though, and that's why we've embraced fake tan/self-tan/sunless tanning – whatever you want to call it.

Right – I'm after doing the serious stuff. You won't hear another peep about it. Check out Chapters 2 and 4 to find out more about sun protection.

THAT'S NEAT: I REALLY LOVE YOUR TIGER FEET

Well, if Mud loved our tiger feet, they were the only feckin' ones. We see it all too often – some bright-orange wan, tangoed to within an inch of her life, but her feet are white or her legs are striped. Sometimes that wan is … me. Or you. What are the most common tan mistakes and how can we avoid them?

Streaks 'n' Stripes

I hate to say it, but any tiger stripes are usually down to poor preparation. Follow the tips for perfect tan application and you should be okay. Basically, make sure you exfoliate properly and give your skin some TLC with loads of moisturiser before even attempting to tan. Blend the product to avoid missing any strategic areas and be especially careful around the shins, knees and feet.

ams
I did my first proper go of St. Tropez Everyday last night. Have a few boo-boos today, particularly on my feet. Note to self: do not apply second layer when drunk tonight.

We've heard many disaster tales following the consumption of a few glasses of wine. Best not to mix alcohol and tan application, so.

Orange Hands

You've got to admit it – this one gets us all at some stage, but it's easy to prevent. If you're using a heavy-duty tan, you absolutely have to wear gloves or apply it with a tan mitt, otherwise it will stain your hands and nails.

Townygirl

I have a photo of me at a wedding and I look quite good until you notice my lovely orange paws wrapped around a glass of wine … classy!

We need to build in a little chant, or mantra if you will, to account for human error: 'After the tan, wash the hands. After the tan wash the hands.' I like to put my mantra to a rap tune, something I could imagine Kanye West or 50 Cent singing. Or maybe not.

Top Tip: Rub a teeny bit of hair serum into the palms of your hands before putting on your tan. It should protect your hands from staining.

OOOMPALOOMPA

Why on earth do we see so many Ooompaloompas in Ireland? Simple: the tans on the market are by and large too dark for us and the shade is often wrong, so a full-strength home tan, or a salon or spray tan, can just look orange and unnatural. That's why gradual tanning can work out so well for lots of us. If you have a horror of looking like one of the weird little people from *Charlie and the Chocolate Factory*, stick to gradual tan.

Shin

One thing that really 'grinds my gears' about fake tan is that some people don't see the need to darken their make-up after painting themselves in tan. No matter how streak-free and perfect their body looks, it's ruined by a big pale head. I refer to it as the Wurzel Gummidge look.

White Side of Boob

Oh lord, White Side of Boob gets me every time. I'll be at an evint, having the wines, getting my picture taken, thinking I look only gorgeous in my new frock and the tan looks OK for once. The next day, the photos go up on the internet for everyone to see – and only then do I realise I've done it again. I was wearing a strappy/sleeveless dress and I forgot to put any tan under my arms. The side of my boobs are much paler than the rest of me. *So* not a good look. Beware.

Acts of God

Sometimes, for no discernable reason, the tan just doesn't come out right. This is obviously an Act of God, an unexplainable event brought about by fate, and there's nothing that can be done about it. The important thing is not to blame yourself in any way.

HOW TO APPLY FAKE TAN

Follow these steps for a light golden glow. Bronze should be the key word, not TK orange.

1. Morning: Exfoliate yourself to the max with a nice moisturising scrub. Get rid of all that yucky dead old skin. Pay special attention to knees and elbows. Slap on lots of body lotion so your skin is nice and hydrated and ready for its brown experience.

2. Evening: You're ready to start tanning. Use the right shade for you. If you're blue-white, use a super light tan. Seriously. You can always put another layer if you're not happy with the colour. If you're a bit more sallow, go for a medium tan. As a very general rule, Irish people should avoid dark tans of any description.

3. Work up from your feet. Make sure you rub it all in as evenly as possible – and watch out for those difficult areas of shins and underarms. Avoid a White Side of Boob situation. Use a mitt for a professional finish!

4. Walk around like John Wayne for a while until it dries in.

Top Tip: Perfect hands are easy! Just wash your hands and then press the backs of your hands against your bum. Voilà! The exact amount of tan will transfer for a perfect colour.

gloss

My absolute fave is Fake Bake. First time, you should get it applied in a salon so that you can see how it's done. Don't even think of buying it without the oil spray. It's about €20 and lasts for months and months. Use it generously on ankles, knees, wrists to avoid horrible orange patches. Latex gloves essential. The downside: it's a lot of work. It has a chocolaty texture. You can't answer the door with it on, and you certainly don't leave the house. You have to stay naked for a while, but it does dry in pretty fast. It doesn't smell great. Your whole bedroom will smell of it the next day. I lie on two sheets when I use it, as it can go through to the mattress. But it washes out of sheets really easily, as the ingredients are all natural and organic. It gives me a beautiful golden tan which lasts about a week. I can't believe I have that much to say about Fake Bake. I do actually have a life – honestly!

If you're leaving it on all night (for St. Tropez or Fake Bake mousse, say) buy a cheap pair of pyjamas from Penneys for the purpose. Otherwise, your sheets will be ruined.

Bingo! You're as cooked as a freshly roasted chicken. And just as delicious.

FIXING MISTAKES

This is a bit hit and miss, to say the least. There are several products on the market that claim to remove streaks (Boots and St. Tropez correcting wipes, for example), but the jury is out on whether they actually work or not. If you don't get to the tan within three hours, you can forget it. And they stink.

Tan is a skin dye, simple as that, so you need to fix the mistake as quickly as possible. Scrubbing your skin won't do it, though it might speed up the fading process. If you can possibly get your hands on some of the stuff hairdressers use to lift hair dye off the skin, that can work, but unless you are a hairdresser, your chances of having a bottle of this handy are pretty slim. Filling in the gaps with bronzer or instant tan may be your best option.

INSTANT TAN

Our conversations on Beaut.ie about fake tan always remind me of the two aul' lads in *The Muppets*. You know the two – Statler and Waldorf, they sit in the balcony box heckling the stage.

Someone will start off recommending a certain brand. 'It's fantastic! The best tan I've ever used in my life!'

Someone else will chip in, 'Well, it's quite good, I suppose.' Then another voice: 'No, it's terrible, the worst tan I've ever used!'

So to allay all this confusion, I will step in as the voice of reason. Here are my recommendations.

littlemisswonders

I had a tan disaster before my Christmas party, and the only thing that would take it off was toothpaste (only lightened it, didn't get rid of it).

Ellie Bellie

Try washing powder mixed with water to form a paste and scrub it with a face cloth. The Vanish powder in the pink tub is particularly good.

Gillian

I've been using the Sally Hansen Airbrush Legs for a while and it's totally fantastic, turns my legs from yucky blue things into normal nice legs! Takes about 10 seconds to apply and then doesn't smudge off at all, it's brilliant.

LanaLamont

The No. 7 lotion is the bee's knees. My body rejects fake tan, it never comes out 100 per cent right. No. 7 is the one I've found the best so far.

Zita

The only tan I ever use is the one LaLa mentioned as the only one she gets away with – No. 7 in light. I'm pale and only use tan on special occasions, but would feel like a right donk if I turned up somewhere with skin five shades darker than usual, so this is perfect. It's inexpensive, application is easy peasy (it's tinted) and it results in a nice, natural colour which doesn't scream 'FAKE TAN ALERT!' It smells good too!

No. 7 Sunless Tanning Quick Dry Tinted Lotion in Light/Medium

The tan that's recommended over and over again for very fair skin on Beaut.ie is No. 7 in Light.

St. Tropez Everyday

I'm a firm fan of St. Tropez Everyday. Great colour and idiot-proof results. It's my favourite gradual tan because it's simply the best. Bettah than all the rest. It gives the most natural colour, it won't streak, it doesn't stink and it's very difficult not to get a good result. Even for the likes of me. Here's how to do it.

1. Apply the tan just like you would a body lotion. Just be more careful to cover all areas. It's colourless on the skin, so the only way you can tell which bits you've done is by the freshly moisturised sheen on your skin. But don't worry about streaks. Because of the way the tan builds up, even if you've made a monumental mistake on Day 1, the other couple of days' application will cancel the boo boo.

2. Repeat the tan application for two more days (skip the body scrub on further days).

3. Now this bit is important: don't keep applying after Day 3, otherwise you'll get a dirty-looking colour. Take a break.

4. Do your scrub again on Day 4 and make sure to use a normal body moisturiser for a couple more days. Then off you go again!

If you like this, you might also like Fake Bake Gradual Self-tanning Lotion.

Fake Bake Fair Gradual Self-tanning Lotion

This is a fantastic gradual tanner and gives a great buildable colour. The mess with regular Fake Bake really puts me off, but like all gradual tanners, this one's a cinch. Try it, you'll like it. Plus, it was formulated for a Celtic skin type. Fancy!

GREEN AND GORGEOUS:
Lavera Self-tanning Lotion

I really love this tan. It actually smells lovely and is jam-packed with gorgeous natural ingredients and not the strong-smelling chemicals that are in so many tans. It's ultra easy to apply, as it's a creamy body lotion-type tan.

Sioux
I am a huge St. Tropez fan. Redhead and freckles, but it has suited me. Try using Bio Oil the night before you put it on to really moisturise, well that and a large glass of vino for a bit of Dutch courage.

Beauty Girl
I use L'Occitane Supple Skin Oil to take off my fake tan. It stops it from going freckly and makes your tan fade nice and evenly.

Gracie
Fake Bake all the way for me. I'm extremely pale, so St. Tropez can look quite dirty on me, but this is a natural-looking tan and even my colleague commented that it was her favourite tan on me. It doesn't stink either – well, not that much anyway – and I quite like using the lotion. Don't feel I get my money's worth with mousse as it seems to go quicker!

BY THE HOKEY

In Asia, skin whitening products enjoy the same popularity that fake tan does here. Seems none of us are ever happy.

Aoife

I have a great fake tan disaster … well, it concerns my dad. When we went away on holidays about 10 years ago to Florida, I brought some fake tan with me. I can't for the life of me remember the name of it, anyway, I left it in the bathroom and my dad mistook it for suntan lotion. He lathered his legs up, good and proper!

We didn't realise his mistake until we were wandering around DisneyLand resort a few hours later and my mum spotted it. It was hilarious. We were all in knots. Dad wasn't amused!

WHY DOES FAKE TAN STINK?

The pleasant-smelling tan you bought in the shop won't smell the same later. Oh no. A chemical in the formula called DHA reacts with skin to make the tan develop, and unfortunately it tends to reek.

To make matters worse, most of us apply our tan before we go to bed, and in bed you get lovely and warm and toasty and your tan develops away during the night.

You'll wake up in the morning smelling like a digestive. Nothing can really be done. Pick a tan that you feel doesn't smell too bad. Your level of tolerance will improve – and the smell doesn't bother some *cailíns*. Much. You have to suffer for beauty, you know.

FACE TAN

Make sure you use a product specially developed for the face. A body tan will clog up your pores and look unnatural. Plus it will be the wrong texture – and shade.

ams
For bad smelly tan, if you can get your hands on some California Tan Neutralizer, it gets rid of 80 per cent of the smell. Your skin smells like something's been cooking on it (i.e. not shower fresh), but it's quite good.

Faces tans are generally lighter than body tans, which is good because it reduces the potential for disaster. However, you always have to be careful. I was going on holiday to the sun once and hadn't had a chance to do anything with my whiteness. I slapped on some Clarins Auto Bronzant for Face. I'd heard great things about this face tan. It's a dark brown liquid that you apply to your face with cotton wool and leave overnight.

Grand. I applied it and then went to bed, setting the alarm for an unholy hour. I got up at 4 a.m. and went into the bathroom to get ready. The face that looked back at me from the mirror didn't look like mine. I was a *much* darker shade than I'd anticipated – the colour of builder's tea.

With no time to do anything more than a quick bit of exfoliation, I had to wait to fix it. That meant hours of hell: queuing in Dublin Airport, a four-hour plane journey and putting up with mucho surprise from those around me. At least the husband got a good laugh out of it.

Lancôme Flash Bronzer

I like Lancôme Flash Bronzer for fast and easy results, though Dove Summer Glow Body Tanning Lotion gets high praise on the Blather.

The Flash Bronzer has a gorgeous mousse texture and you can actually see it going on (unlike most tans that take a while to develop and usually result in me missing several strategic areas). And it smells fine. That's where a lot of fake tan falls down – the reeking. This one leaves me with a gorgeous glow.

Hamilton Tru Bronze

An absolute gem, Tru Bronze is one of those little secrets hidden away on the shelves in the chemists. Using walnut extract, it gives an even, smooth, streak-free finish. Doesn't smell horrible and doesn't turn you orange, this stuff will give the tanorexics amongst you something to smile about. Oh, and it's really well priced.

PRODUCTS OF YORE: Rimmel Sun Shimmer

My sister swears by Sun Shimmer! She mixes it with moisturiser and it looks really natural, plus it showers off. An extra bonus is that it boasts a Price of Yore, too.

Spray Tan and Salon Tans

These are great for a quick fix – just make sure you pick a pale shade, as spray tan has a terrible tendency to look far too orange.

Salon tans (like St. Tropez or Decléor, applied by a therapist) generally look the most natural, so try to choose these.

Jen
Don't like spray tans. I have big boobs and find that the spray does not go under them completely, so if wearing bikini you have a light white crescent. Not an option. Normally apply it myself.

Salon Secrets

Gemma, an ex beauty therapist, told me about setting up a room in her home to do spray tans, nails, that kind of thing.

'This woman came in one evening for a tan. I gave her the paper G-string and I left the room while she got undressed and put on the disposable. She called me when she was ready and in I went. She had the G-string on the wrong way around. I didn't say a word, just sprayed her.'

9

Mane Attraction

...WAYS TO NOURISH AND PROTECT HAIR, KEEP IT SUPER SMOOTH AND SHINY AND FIND OUT WHAT THE EXPERTS RECOMMEND...

Gruaig a Go Go

Hair care is something we spend so much time and money on. Wash your hair with the wrong shampoo and it's like a Brillo pad. Or a lank greaseball. Or dull. Or has no volume. And that's why this chapter is all about ways to nourish and protect hair, keep it super smooth and shiny and find out what the experts recommend.

But let's start with the basics – shampoo and conditioner. You need to get the right ones or you'll never have a good hair day.

Spend on a Good Shampoo

A lot of people quail at the thought of spending more than a fiver on a bottle of shampoo or conditioner. But if you can justify spending on clothes or shoes, then it makes sense that you can also do this with hair care. After all, your hair is with you all the time and is a reflection of your personality. Those shoes, on the other hand, gorgeous as they may be, will see more of the inside of the wardrobe than anything else.

My pick is the Kérastase brand because it's the one that's done it for me time and time again. I also like the fact that there are ranges to suit all hair types and conditions. Hairdressers refer to Kérastase as the Gucci of hair care and I think that once you've used it and loved it, you'll never go back to supermarket brands.

There's no denying that salon brands are more expensive, but they do usually last for ages (you only need to use a tiny amount). In fact, once you find a brand that works for you, it's like the beginning of a long love affair. I like to share my love around, though, and I also really like

Redken's Smooth Down range for dry, frizzy manes; Wella System Professional's line of Luminous shampoo and conditioners, which add great shine to hair; Bumble and Bumble and Shu Uemura's Art of Hair shampoo and conditioners.

So this is how I work the value for money bit. You will get X number of washes out of a bottle of shampoo. Divide this into the price of the bottle of shampoo and you get the price per wash, which will be a few cents. And to make it even cheaper, I buy the huge salon-size bottles – one litre of Kérastase lasts a hell of a long time.

Expensive shampoo is like Fairy Liquid, you see: a little goes a loooong way. A litre of shampoo may feel like fair whack to shell out for in one go, but trust me, it will save you a fortune, and you won't need to buy any more shampoo for months and months. Ka-ching!

SUPERMARKET FAVOURITES

While I'll happily admit to being a posh hair-care girl, there are some good products out there that don't cost half a month's rent. Colet Earth is a great line of naturals-based products that are kind to hair and Yes to Carrots shampoo and conditioners come in great big bottles, are brilliant value and don't add much build-up. If you're particularly sensitive of scalp, check out La Roche-Posay's Kerium line, as it's fab for people who find that ordinary shampoo irritates their delicate skin. Garnier Herbal Essences will give you a great head of shiny hair that smells delicious. As an added bonus, you'll also have an orgasm in the shower every time you use it .... apparently.

Let's look at the less expensive brands too and see which ones are rated.

Bunnybun
I don't believe in spending big bucks on shampoo, as I wash my hair every day and go through it too fast. I am loving Aussie, the clarifying one and the moisturising one and of course the 3 Minute Miracle mask.

Poppins
Anything from the Aussie range is excellent. I often use this brand to take a break from my Kérastase.

Jenizzle
Aussie shampoos and conditioners – Colour Mate Shampoo is the only shampoo anyone with coloured hair should go near. It keeps my pink (yes, PINK!) hair super shiny and healthy, even after a bleaching and re-dying session. 3 Minute Miracle conditioner saved my hair forever.

Hen
The James Brown range in Boots is fab. I totally only bought it because Kate Moss is the face of it, but it really is fantastic. I got the shampoo, conditioner (better than most high-end ones), serum and hairspray and have not been disappointed with one of them. And it's very good value too!

USES FOR SHAMPOOS AND CONDITIONERS YOU DON'T LIKE

- Wash your animals with it.
- Use it to shave your legs.
- Give it to the man in your life.

THE LOWDOWN ON SILICONE

Silicone is an ingredient present in most shampoos and is great for making your hair shiny and smooth. But too much of it will weigh your hair down and eventually make it look flat and dull. Silicone-heavy shampoos have great results at first – making many people believe they are the bee's knees – but after a while, build-up can cause damage.

Phyto is a high-quality range of French hair care that uses botanicals, essential oils and active ingredients. It aims to actually treat the problems particular hair types have instead of just masking them like regular hair care ranges. Other no-silicone or low-silicone ranges include Aveda, Burt's Bees, Dr. Hauschka, L'Occitane, Lavera and Weleda.

One of the key aspects of the Phyto range is the lack of silicones, detergents or salts, which can cause damage to hair in the long term. Sounds great, but be warned: it's not that simple. Switching from a silicone-rich shampoo to a silicone-free shampoo can lead to weeks of frizzy, horrible hair.

My advice? Silicone is present in most shampoos and it's not anything to get too hung up about. If you do want to try to avoid silicone, go for the natural ranges like Phyto and avoid Pantene, Fructis and other silicone-heavy shampoos.

Marie

I switched to Phyto. You have to be strong, because during one month or so you will see your real hair all damaged by the silicone and not hidden by the silicone any more.

Kirstie

Silicones aren't bad in themselves, in fact they're often used for hydration in moisturisers, but it's just that they can really build up on hair and cause it to feel lank after a while. Great for smoothing frizz though, which is why they're in so many styling products.

Miss_M

Lush has some great shampoos and conditioners that don't contain silicones and their prices are also pretty decent. I really like their Rehab Shampoo and Ultimate Shine solid bar shampoo.

TIPS FOR OILY OR GREASY HAIR

The temptation to go for harsh shampoos is one you should resist. One of the best features of hair is its washability, so wash your hair frequently (once a day if you have to) with a gentle shampoo. If your hair is long, don't forget that the ends of it can get dry even if it's oily up top, so use conditioner on the ends.

CB

I love dry shampoo! It's the best rescue ever on the occasional day that I get up too late to have a shower. It smells a bit funny but does the trick. I have Lee Stafford dry shampoo that I got in Boots.

minxinparis

Another good dry shampoo is Klorane, a bit pricey though.

Dry shampoo comes into its own with your hair type. It absorbs excess oil and it's worth a try for those days when you didn't get a chance to lather up.

The Drys to Try

Good old Batiste is on hand for every day. Spray it into roots and it'll instantly banish oil and lankness, giving you another day out of a wash. It's also excellent for adding volume to limp hair and can be used as a first step before styling, too. Cheap and reliable.

A more expensive option, but better for those with particularly fine hair, are Bumble and Bumble's hair powders. They come in coloured versions, so you can match one to your own shade.

James Brown Combination Hair Shampoo

Most oily girls find it's only their roots that get really bad, so James Brown's Combination Shampoo is perfect for hydrating ends and removing grease.

TIPS FOR NORMAL HAIR

If you've got normal hair, then thank your lucky stars.

- Stay as far away from harsh colouring treatments and styling as you can.
- Wash with a mild shampoo.
- Never scrub the ends of your hair together when washing (this goes for everyone), and never let a hairdresser do it either.
- Don't stuff it into ponytails (this breaks the hair and damages it).
- Get it trimmed regularly to keep it free from split ends.
- Let it dry naturally as much as possible.

Normal Necessities

You're lucky – you can use a wide range of products, and you'll probably find that you're the type best suited to trying organic and silicone-free shampoos, which can cause other types to go a bit haywire.

Gorgeous Shampoo and Conditioner

Aveda Rosemary Mint Shampoo and Conditioner are ideal for you. Packed full of yummy ingredients like organic lavender, these products are gentle enough to use every day, while leaving hair sweet smelling and clean.

Styling Tip

If you use a hairdryer or straighteners often, then you'll want to mind your nice, normally behaving hair so it doesn't dry out on you. GHD Obedience Cream is great for pre-heat styling and will add protection and gloss.

TIPS FOR CURLY HAIR

As a curly girl myself, maybe I'm going to be a bit biased in what I say here, but in my honest opinion, curly hair is the most difficult of all the hair types to manage. It is wayward, very dry and needs all the help it can get. So here's a few tips and products we've found good for avoiding the freshly blow-dried poodle look.

The Disturbing Tale of My Curly Hair

One morning I woke up. My hair was curly.

It felt like it literally happened overnight, but obviously the telltale signs had been there for some time: more and more struggling with the hair dryer to get it smooth and straight. More and more hair serums being purchased, tried and discarded in disgust because they 'didn't work'. A need for more and more high-quality shampoos and conditioners.

But the writing was on the wall. The hair was going curly. I know not why, after years of being relatively straight and well behaved, it suddenly decided to turn itself into a nasty furze bush. It took me some time to come to terms with it – hence the self-denial mentioned in the previous paragraph. Having spent the 1980s getting my hair permed because it was too straight (and as you know, girls, you couldn't hold your head up in school without your shag perm), I was now spending the Noughties getting it straightened.

However, once accepted, I took steps to make the best of the curly situation. Curly hair is really dry, and for me that had to mean the end of highlights, no more straighteners, blow-drying reserved only for special occasions and Kérastase Oleo Relax became the only shampoo range allowed near The Hair. Various curl controllers and frizz reducers were tried, but none of them got the gold seal or got accepted into the hair staple stable.

Try some of these products if you too are struggling with your furze bush. The one on your head, I mean.

AISLING'S PICK: Aveda
Be Curly Curl Enhancer

Truly, it is Most Excellent. You apply the deliciously fresh-smelling Curl Enhancer cream generously to wet hair and allow it to dry naturally or blow-dry with a diffuser if you want more volume. Your hair will be glossy, shiny, smell great and your curls will be beautifully defined. It seems to work best on thicker hair though, so if yours is quite fine, it might not suit you.

The Bumble and Bumble Curl Conscious range is fantastic, too. 'Changed my life', one curly girl told me, and she wasn't exaggerating.

Meluia

I have very dry, thick and fuzzy curly hair. I find curling anti-frizz products dry it out a lot, so now I use hair conditioner to curl my hair. Aussie 3 Minute Miracle is the best of the lot. I use the long hair one. Put it into wet hair then scrunch dry and it gives you non-frizzy curls and your hair smells lovely too.

Fiona

Be Curly is quite simply THE best curl treatment I have found in literally years of trying every damn curl product on the market for my very curly, frizz-prone mop. It's pricey, but even on a limited budget it is 100 per cent worth it. I cannot recommend it enough.

lippy loo

I've curly hair, and Be Curly is one of the very few (years of trying) products that I like. The Be Curly Shampoo and Conditioner are also lovely.

By The Hokey

Redheads actually have less hair on their heads compared to other hair colours. On average, a redser will have 90,000 hairs compared to a blonde's 140,000. Don't know what that's got do with the price of spuds, but sure, I thought I'd tell yiz anyway.

Tips for Fine and Flyaway Hair

Fine and flyaway hair needs a light touch. Use a shampoo specifically formulated for your hair type – regular shampoo will be too heavy and make it look lank and greasy. Sunsilk has good products for fine hair.

Dee

I had an abundance of split ends and my hair is really thin, so it was quite damaged and flyaway. I used to have loads of hairs sticking up everywhere as soon as I finished blow-drying! Then I started using Aussie Long and Luscious leave-in conditioner. Wash your hair, spray in, comb through and leave it. And my hair has honestly never been better! And it's really not that expensive … bit of a bargain!

Don't use mousse to add volume – it's too heavy for you. Use one of the new volumising sprays instead, like L'Oréal Professionnel Serie Expert Volume Expand Root Lift Spray. Or try Bumble and Bumble Thickening Spray (smells delicious too!).

Never use conditioner the whole way through your hair. Use it only on the mid-lengths and ends – and sparingly at that. Too many highlights are a disaster for you, as they thin your hair even further. I know it's hard, but try to cut down!

Best Shampoo and Conditioner

Protein-enriched shampoos are brilliant for this hair type, as they can penetrate the follicle and add plumpness to hair – and that's what you want. Check out Frederic Fekkai's deadly Protein Rx range, which your hair will drink up.

Fine Hair Styling

You need something to smooth down flyaways and add shine. Redken's Smooth Down Sleek Obedience solid serum would be a good bet – just go easy on it, as product can really weigh your fine hair down.

Top Tip: When using a styling product like wax or pomade, remember, less really is more for your hair type. Scoop out a tiny piece and massage into the palms. When it's melted and pliable, work through the hair using your hands.

Top Tip: Try giving fine hair a light blow-dry the second day after washing. This will give it a lift and revive the style.

trillian

The only time I didn't wash my hair every day/second day was after I got super blonde highlights by mistake. I think the girl who was doing the colour forgot about me and left the dye in too long, but my hair was like straw afterwards.

TIPS FOR COLOURED HAIR

Your hair will look and feel brilliant immediately after you've had your colour done – and then it starts to go downhill. Coloured hair fades, splits, feels rough and in general behaves badly. Try using colour-enhancing shampoos and conditioners in between hair appointments.

Condition, condition, condition. Treat your hair to regular masks, wrapping hair in a warm towel to open the cuticles of the hair, which aids absorption of care products.

Ranges that contain sunscreens can work really well for you, as sunlight is the main culprit in the auld fading problem.

Also Recommended: Bumble and Bumble Thickening Spray and James Brown Dry Shampoo.

Zita

I'm a big John Frieda fan too. Frizz-Ease is a godsend. The Serum Finishing Spray has been a can't-live-without product of mine for years and years. I love the Brilliant Brunette range too – it definitely adds warmth to my dark locks. The colour glaze is a three-minute treatment with pigment that I was initially a bit dubious about, as such things can be a bit messy and crap. However, while it doesn't, er, 'glaze' my hair as promised, I've found that using it in conjunction with the Brilliant Brunette shampoo and conditioner leaves my hair looking rather marvellous. Hurray for John Frieda.

John Frieda Blow Dry Lotion

Use this pre-blow-drying for lift at the roots.

Great Sun Protection Range

Kérastase Soleil is great for saving coloured hair from the ravages of the sun's rays on a daily basis, as well as protecting when you're on your holliers. It's not too likely that you'll be subject to sun, sea water and chlorine on the average Irish day, but if colour-fade is a big problem, then lash a bit of Kérastase Soleil Voile Protecteur on when you know you'll be out and about a lot. Also try L'Oréal Elvive Colour Protect – great range, great price.

 AISLING'S PICK: John Frieda Brilliant Brunette

There's a John Frieda product for every type of hair: thick, thin, limp, curly or frizzy. And guess what? They all work. It's a high-street brand that's affordable, highly effective and comes in enough formats to suit every hair type.

First there's the fabulous Frizz-Ease serum, of course, and even this comes in three strengths, depending on the thickness and, er, frizz of your hair. A few drops of this serum applied to wet hair can tame even the most difficult to blow-dry hair, and I speak from experience here. My hair has a mind of its own, it does what it wants and it never seems to do what I want, but Frizz-Ease helps smoothen it dramatically. The Frizz-Ease range contains all sorts of other goodies too: shampoos, conditioners and treatments.

Next up is the Brilliant Brunette range, which I just love too. Shampoos, conditioners, glosses, hairsprays, serums, shiners, mousses, goop to tame curly hair … and of course there's the same fab ranges for you blondes and redheads too (Sheer Blonde and Radiant Red).

MAMMY SAYS

Ah girls, will ye get away with all this fancy talk of frenchy shampoos and conditioners! Sure, isn't it all just suds in the end? A good scrub with a bar of coal tar soap keeps it clean for days and days. Condition? I don't worry myself about that at all. Keep it nice and short. It doesn't do at all at all to be having long hair once you're past 25, that's for young wans. You don't want to be lookin' like the Banshee from the Fairy Ring. Mona from the post office saw her last year. She's not been right since, God love her. I throw in a few Hail Marys for her every night.

TIPS FOR DRY HAIR

Alas, this is the type of hair that many of us have. Sun, colouring, heat styling and just pure years passing mean hair gets thinner and drier. Conditioners, intensive conditioners and hair masks are all necessary to keep dry hair soft and shiny, and there are lots of natural alternatives too that don't cost the earth and work really well. Styling products and leave-in conditioners can be used to very good effect to keep everything looking cared for.

- Use a shampoo and conditioner specifically for dry hair.
- Anything with shea, coconut or any kind of 'butter' will be good for your hair.
- In the name of god, don't heat style too much. Give your hair a break every second wash and let it dry naturally.

- Slather on an intensive mask at least once a week.

- Lightening the hair (with highlights, for example) is terrible for dry hair.

- Use an overnight hair conditioner to give it an extra boost.

- If your hair is ultra dry and you're fighting every day to make it look smooth and sleek – cut it. Sorry, but it's for the best.

- The organic and natural ranges are winners when it comes to dry hair. Anything with natural oils and creams will do your hair a world of good. Their ingredients will actually penetrate the hair shaft to deep-down condition – unlike the mass market ranges, which may just coat the hair with silicone to make it appear smoother.

L'Occitane Shea Butter

A scrummy range containing gorgeous products for dry hair. Rich, creamy and delicious, the Ultra Rich Shampoo and Ultra Rich Conditioner are brilliant and will leave even the crunchiest of hair soft and smooth.

Body Shop Brazil Nut Moisture Mask

With brazil nut, olive and sesame oils, Body Shop Brazil Nut Moisture Mask will penetrate your hair to leave it deep-down soft. Leave on overnight for even more power-packed richness.

OVERNIGHT HAIR CONDITIONERS

Products like Kérastase's Noctogenist range, Umberto Giannini Overnight Beauty Moisture Balm and Frizz-Ease Crème Serum Overnight Repair Formula all work as an overnight moisturising treatment for hair. Just think of them like a night cream – for your locks. Don't overload your hair with cream, just apply to the ends and dry parts. In the morning you'll wake up with softer, smoother hair that smells gorgeous. No need to wash, just go. A cheaper option is L'Oréal Paris' Elvive Re-Nutrition Night Serum.

Go Au Naturel with Neem

No, I'm not talking about *that* kind of au naturel: whipping off your tankini on the beach in Courttown. Though you can if you like, for who knows the steps fate may take? A burly guard may be dispatched urgently to cover you with a towel and take the opportunity to arrange a date by the waltzers later that night. Jesus, he might even stand you a single of chips and a bottle of Coors Light. If you're very lucky.

What I was actually going to tell you about was neem oil. Fantastic stuff. I can't say enough good things about it. Hair drinks it in and emerges revitalised. Try it, you'll be converted. Dr. Hauschka's Neem Hair Oil lasts for ages and ages.

A word of warning, though: I've found that it does seem to fade my coloured hair, so now I only use the oil just before I'm getting it coloured anyway.

Home Hair Colour: the Recessionista's Choice

The popularity of home hair colour is most definitely on the rise. It's cheap, there is a huge choice available, and yes, you can really cover greys. Boxes of colour are flying off the shelves as more and more of you are opting to either colour at home exclusively, or to eke out your salon visits by alternating them with home colour.

Here are the pros and cons of those boxes of home hair colour:

PROS

Price

It's obviously so much cheaper to colour your hair yourself, so that's very appealing in these credit-crunch times.

Good results

The formulations of home hair colour have improved so much recently that it's easier to colour at home and get good, long-lasting results.

Time

If you're like me then you feel that two hours in a salon chair getting your colour topped up is two hours of your life you're never gonna get back. (Yes, the magazines and the coffee do go a long way towards making up for that, though.) Home hair colour can now work in ten minutes, which is a definite plus in its favour.

Range of shades

The variety of shades now available is massive and most of them are formulated to cover greys – just check the label.

Root top-up

Between salon visits I'll admit I have resorted to the old trick* of mascara to touch up those roots. (*Just for the record this is a rubbish trick.) But if you've got half an inch of re-growth showing and no time to get to the hairdresser, a root top-up product will be an absolute life saver for you.

Cons

Mess

No getting around the fact that home hair dye can make a mess: it tends to drip (no matter what Davina or Andie say), and can splatter all over your bathroom. The dark shades are the most dangerous, so exercise extreme caution (especially if you've got long hair). But provided you're very careful, use old towels and wear a horrible old t-shirt that you're not afraid to ruin you'll probably be okay.

Stink

If you're remembering the Hair Colours of Yore then you can remember the eye-watering stink. The new creams are formulated so that the smelly ingredients are minimised and because they work faster, you won't have to endure it for long.

Hairdressers don't like them

Hairdressers aren't keen on seeing you with a headful of patchy dye and having to sort it out. For one, they don't know exactly what chemicals were in the colour you used and how it will react with their products. So tear out the label and keep it to show them.

Nobody does it better

Be warned though: it's highly unlikely that you're going to match salon results at home. They're the experts after all.

Top Tips:

- Put a thick layer of Vaseline or face cream around your hairline to stop the colour dying your skin.

- Long hair will most probably need two packs of colour. Don't skimp on the amount you apply or you're likely to end up with an uneven or patchy colour.

- For the love of God, don't attempt to go more than one or two shades darker or lighter at home. Go to the hairdresser and get professional advice before you commit to a drastic shade change.

- If you hate the colour, wash it out immediately with washing up liquid. The detergents can help to strip out colour.

Great Picks for Home Hair Colour
Permanent

Nice and Easy by Clairol is the perennial favourite for covering grey and restoring lustre to faded shades.

Root Touch-up

Clairol Nice and Easy Perfect 10.

Vibrant

L'Oreal Feria – permanent shades particularly good for rich reds. Definite vavavoom.

Quick and Easy

Garnier Herbashine. Formulated to be less harsh (contains no ammonia) and works in ten minutes. Brilliant.

John Frieda Luminous Colour Glaze

Designed to enhance your natural colour and make it temporarily more intense.

HAIR LOVES HEALTH

Ah, hair can't survive on a diet of Bacardi Breezers and Tayto. More's the pity. Oh no, hair just has to love health, doesn't it? Pesky hair.

You can be slathering on as many expensive products as you like, but if you're not feeding it right, it's never gonna look its best.

Hair is strict and in a nun-like fashion it loves to be fed on a nutritious, healthy diet of green veg, water and chastity. (OK, I made that last one up.) Hair loves protein, so feed it good-quality stuff. Fish and eggs are particularly good. Brown rice, wheat germ, avocado, pulses and loads of fruit and veg will give it the vitamins and minerals it needs. Crash dieting is a disaster for the auld *gruaig*, so make sure to shlurp down a few yoghurts and other moo products even when trying to lose weight. For the calcium, like.

As an added bonus, any regime that you embark on for the hair will also show in your nails. They're made of the same stuff, you see. But be patient. It will take a few months to see results. No instant gratification here. Bah!

littlemisswonders
Oh god … Hint of a Tint … I destroyed our bathroom with that … and also a lot of my clothes too … and my forehead … basically I shouldn't be let near anything that alters colours.

Errol's girl
Jesus I remember Sun-In turned my brown hair yellow and made it go frizzy. I pretended to my friends that it was sun-bleached even though it had lashed rain all summer and I'd only got as far as Wexford! Henna – oh, the smell and the powder didn't mix properly so your hair came out all patchy and it dyed your bathroom including the grouting and the floor … sigh!

Pearl
I've taken Perfectil in the past and haven't noticed any difference (I have very weak nails). I did hear Imeeden was good. At that price, it should be!

CELEB BEAUTY SECRETS:
Catherine Zeta Jones

There aren't many women who seem to have it all, but Catherine Zeta Jones looks like she might be one of them. Drop-dead gorgeous, fantastic figure, movie stardom … oh, and Michael Douglas. Still, you can't have everything, can you?

Then there's the hair. CZJ has the most beautiful, thick glossy mane imaginable. While the rest of us make do with a quick lather with the auld Elvive, perhaps treating it to a deep condition once a week, CJZ slathers hers with Beluga caviar.

Yes, caviar. OMG, how yuck does that sound? It's a treatment that lasts about two hours and costs a bleedin' fortune. Probably. CZJ relaxes with a glass of champers as her hair is washed with truffle shampoo. Truffle shampoo … hokay. Then the liquidised fish eggs are spread on her hair, combed through and – this is the truly horrible bit – left to set. But she loves it, apparently. I think I would be sick. And then at the end of it she has to go home to the craether.

Harto

I take a multivitamin, vitamin B, vitamin C and omega 3 capsules every day. I started taking them for health reasons, but I think my skin, hair and nails have improved since starting. If I'm off them for any length of time, my nails start to break and my skin starts looking crappy. I keep them on my desk in work and it reminds me to take them every day.

DIARY OF A BAD HAIR DAY

Friday 13th An apposite date to be having a bad hair day, I suppose.

7 a.m. Alarm goes off. Hit the snooze button, roll back over to continue delicious dream involving Jonathan Rhys Myers.

7:10 Alarm goes off. Hit the snooze button again. Daniel Craig now involved in dream also.

7:20 Feckin' alarm finally shrieks through to conscious mind. Violently silence it and doze another 10 minutes before finally throwing back the duvet.

7:30 Stumble into bathroom. Catch sight of hair in mirror. Like something from *Bridget Jones's Diary*, it has transformed itself into some horrible creation of peaks and troughs overnight. I went to bed with my hair still damp the night before and it took the opportunity to rebel against me. No time to wash it now, panic sets in.

7:45 Three cats cross my path. On a day like today, that should be lucky, but none of them are black and all of them are clamouring noisily to be fed. Spoon Whiskas into bowls and root out the hair straighteners. Breaking all my own rules, I know, but this is an EMERGENCY! Blast hair with GHD Iron Oil (don't know if this stuff works, but I use it as a talisman against the evil ravages of the straighteners).

7:50 Marginally better. A few squirts of John Frieda smoothing balm stuff and it will have to do.

7:55 Mad late now.

8:01 In car at last, traffic bumper to bumper on the M50; chew a piece of cold toast. Meeting with The Boss first thing and I'm still not over my hair trauma. Catch sight of myself in the rear view mirror, it's not pretty.

Spend the whole day hating hair, going into the loos at every opportunity to wet bits of it, use all the random serums and other hair stuff that I keep in my desk drawer, to no avail. In the end, constrain it into a severe ponytail, clip back the front part and resign myself to looking like crap.

DIY: Conditioner

I'm happy to report that there was no need for Teddy's intervention in this chapter, as we have plenty of money-saving recipes ourselves. We've put everything from mayonnaise to honey in our hair to condition it. One of the best tips we got was from Glitterkitty, a frequent Blatherer. She told us that coconut oil is only fabilis for adding shine and lustre to hair. You can buy a big tub of it in the chemist – it's really cheap – and you simply warm 2 teaspoons up in your hands (use more or less depending on the length of your hair). Spread it through hair and recline, preferably reading trashy magazines, for a couple of hours. Shampoo out and you're good to go.

Hot Oil

1. Take an oil like olive or coconut and put a couple of teaspoons in a sandwich bag.

2. Dip the bag in a cup of hot water for a couple of minutes to heat up the oil.

3. Spread through your hair with your fingers, paying particular attention to the ends.

4. Pile your hair on top of your head and wrap it in clingfilm. Leave it on for as long as you can – overnight if you want – before shampooing out.

5. *Voilà* – lovely glossy locks. This works just as well as any shop-bought hot oil treatment and is much cheaper.

Makeupstuff

In India, women have used coconut oil as a pre-wash treatment for many, many years. Oil treatments are really common there. Coconut oil is the best hair oil. It has been proven that coconut oil reduced protein loss in hair when washing.

sweetie

Coconut oil is brilliant for conditioning the *gruaig*. Lash some on at night, comb through and wash hair in the morning. I just do it once a week on the ends only cos I've greasy hair, but it really conditions. Also massaging it into the nails too really strengthens them.

Em

For years I've used olive oil on my hair. My grandmother recommended it to me when I was about 13, apparently it was something my great-grandmother always used on her hair. I rub it in, leave it on overnight (making sure I've covered my pillow with a towel) and then wash it out in the morning. I have a dry scalp and it really helps with that, plus my hair is so much more manageable and shiny and my hairdresser even remarked about my hair being in better condition. I use Boots Skin Softening Olive Oil, which is about the same price as the coconut oil. It works better than any of the conditioners I've tried.

Ms Sittingatherdeskandpretendingtowork

To shine hair, I boil some rosemary in a litre of water. Once cold, you can use this as your final rinse. It really does work – takes a few weeks now. You should leave the rosemary in the bottle. It does look like a spider though – gives me the creeps sometimes.

Jules

I used to have a terrible addiction to getting my hair highlighted and it was really only cured when several hairdressers flatly refused to put any more colour in my hair because it was so damaged and broken. Over the past year, I've been so good to my hair – gone is the GHD, I only use the green Kérestase and I've been taking vitamin B complex. It all seems to be working and my hair is in much better condition and doesn't fall out in clumps any more when I brush it. I have to say it though – there's a huge buzz from getting your hair coloured and I'm dying to get it done again!

WORK OF SATAN: Hair Straighteners

Oh, dear. I know so many of us love them, but they are A Very Bad Idea for hair. Nothing will dry and frazzle it so quickly. The heat is intense and it's being applied directly to hair. You might feel you're getting away with it for now, but honestly, as your teacher used to say coming up to your Junior Cert mocks, 'You're only fooling yourself.'

Instant gratification usually ain't worth it. Lecture over.

10

Ace of Base

THE ONE THAT GIVES YOU FLAWLESS COVERAGE, YET STILL LOOKS LIKE YOUR OWN SKIN....

There's no doubt about it, foundation is a terrible fecker of a product to buy. I bet you've gone through tons of different kinds in an effort to find one that suits you. You know – the ONE.

The one that gives you flawless coverage, yet still looks like your own skin. That gives you a luminous radiant glow. That is exactly – and I mean exactly – the right shade. And did I mention that it would be great if it made you look like a supermodel? But you accept that this might be pushing it a bit too far.

Now this is one of the few areas where you get what you pay for. As you've seen, my philosophy is to choose what works and that there are plenty of brilliant low-priced products out there in other areas of beauty. But I have to change my tune a bit when it comes to foundation. Spend on your foundation, because buying a quality base really is worth it. It will give you better coverage, it will look more natural and last longer. People will ask you where you got your foundation 'cos it looks so goddamn good.

A caveat: teenagers can get away with just about anything and your Saturday job in the newsagents won't stretch to Armani. Ditto students. You need your money for parties and laptop batteries, so we'll have a look at what's best in the less-expensive ranges too.

There's nothing better than getting your foundation right. And of course the opposite is true too: there's no beauty boo-boo worse than getting it wrong.

FOUNDATION BUYING GUIDE

STEP ONE Be prepared for the long haul. It's unlikely that you will find your perfect foundation straight away. Oh, did I say unlikely? I meant Mission Impossible. Do your research. Go online, read magazines, ask people with gorgeous foundation what they're using.

STEP TWO Now remember: the fluorescent lighting in department stores or chemists does not, I repeat does not, give you any sort of idea of what your foundation will look like in real life. Neither will testing a shade on your wrist. You need to see the shade on your face in a variety of lights. This means you must get made up in store, or get samples. Preferably both.

STEP THREE Go into the shop with no make-up on whatsoever. Go to your chosen make-up counter and tell them what you're looking for. (Perhaps you need foundation that will increase radiance, not settle into lines, suitable for oily skin or with medium coverage, for example). You may have a recommendation already, but keep schtum – see what the sales assistant suggests and keep an open mind.

STEP FOUR Now get the foundation applied. Resist the urge to get pretty blushers and bronzers plonked on top – the beauty counter wants you to spend as much as possible and will tempt you like a devil on your shoulder. But remain strong. If you get these products applied, you won't be able to see the effect of the foundation properly. Now you must leave. Do not purchase yet. Simply say that you need to see the foundation in natural light.

STEP FIVE Actually see the foundation in natural light. Walk around – meet your sister or a pal for lunch and see what she thinks. Don't bother asking your boyfriend or husband, because they won't understand the seriousness of the question and will only grunt, 'Yeah, it's grand.'

- If you love the foundation – hurrah! Back you go and buy it.
- If you hate the foundation – the coverage, the consistency and so on – it's time to strike that one off your list. The search must resume with a different brand.
- If you like the texture and coverage of the foundation but think that the shade is wrong, then just go back and ask for samples in a different shade. Which brings us on to the next point…

STEP SIX Beauty counters are notoriously stingy about giving out foundation samples. This is ridiculous. How on earth can you be expected to shell out for something that you must wear on your face every day and you've never even had a chance to try? Get with the programme, cosmetics companies. Meanwhile, be ready for their excuses.

Bring your own little sample jars with you. All you want is a teeny amount – enough for one make-up application. It's not going to bring Estée Lauder to its knees, for christsakes. Insist nicely on getting it.

Top Ten Base Desires

Everyone's skin is different and everyone expects different things from their foundation. Because of this, it's impossible to say categorically which ones are best. But there are some foundations that are brought up time and time again as being superb. Want to know what we rate? Read on!

1. Full Coverage: Estée Lauder Double Wear

Estée Lauder Doublewear is beloved of ladies who are keen to cover up every single blemish. It's great for big nights out and those television appearances we all have to contend with. 'Cos trust me – there's no way any studio light is gonna find a blemish behind this stuff. Doublewear stays put, and then some. So if you've got oily skin and find your foundation slides off in a couple of hours, give this a try. And for those of you who like the sound of this but would prefer lighter coverage, you can get your paws on Double Wear Light.

2. Long-lasting: Clinique Superfit Makeup

Reformulated and now better than ever, Clinique's Superfit Makeup is a bit of a classic. Designed to last all day, this stuff stays put. Great for sebum-prone skin types, as it's oil free.

3. Personalised Base: Prescriptives Custom Blend

The options are almost endless with Prescriptives Custom Blend service. Foundation (and concealer) can be created to precisely match

Gilly

I got that Custom Blend foundation from Prescriptives a few weeks ago and love it – perfect colour match for my skin, good coverage, good staying power and good for my dry skin. It's pretty expensive, but you get loads and I think it's well worth it for having such a good match to my skin. Another good thing is that if you get it home and think it's not quite right, you can bring it back in and get them to make it lighter, darker or more moisturising, etc.

your skin tone – totally deadly if you're pale as a pooka and no other brand can match your particular pallor. There's no arguing with the fact that it's expensive, but they can really tailor this for all your needs: coverage, shade and moisturisation can all be adjusted just for you.

4. Mix It Up: Revlon Custom Creations

Revlon are on to a winner with their Custom Creations Foundation. An idea similar to the Prescriptives concept, there are six shades available, each of which can be further customised into five shades at the twist of a dial. Brilliant when you've just been on holliers, have a bit of an auld tan and don't want to splash the cash on a new product.

Bee

The girl in Armani looked at me strangely when I asked her to apply the Luminous Silk, but I wanted to wear it for the day before deciding. She seemed a bit miffed when I asked for a tester of it and could she write down the products she used. Granted, it was a Saturday in Brown Thomas Dublin and they were busy, but isn't that what they're there for?

5. Oily Skin Types: Chanel Mat Lumière

Dry types, this will screech across your skin like nails on a blackboard, but you sebum-prone lassies will swoon for Chanel's Mat Lumière base. Firmly damping down shine, it gives a matte finish to skin and lasts. And lasts. Expensive, but worth the splurge if you're tearing your hair out trying to find a product to suit your skin.

6. Mid-Price Marvel: Max Factor Lasting Performance

Make-up artists love Max Factor and so do we. Lasting Performance has been around for donkey's years and I still reach for it when I run out of whatever posh base I've been spoiling myself with. Like the name says, it stays put, comes in a good shade range and looks nice and natural.

7. Great Skin Glow

There are two I'd recommend for night-time. If you've got great skin, lash on the Giorgio Armani Luminous Silk with impunity, as it's a sheer, glam base that reflects light and works wonders on already great skin. If you want a little more coverage, then check out Lancôme's Photogenic Lumessence foundation. A similar look and feel to the Armani product, it gives more cover.

8. Oh So Easy: YSL Perfect Touch

With its smart little built-in brush, Yves Saint Laurent's Perfect Touch Brush Foundation is fierce handy altogether. Delivering dewy medium coverage, all you need to do is turn on to dispense, paint your face and bob's your uncle. Just remember one thing, though – you need to run the brush under the tap every now and then or it'll go a bit smelly.

cathyfly

I've often been tempted to try out a certain foundation on the recommendation of a friend, but it can be hit and miss as everyone's skin is so different. For example, I swear by my Chanel Vitalumière fluid, which I've been using for a few years now, and have a friend who loves the Giorgio Armani Luminous Silk and her skin always looks amazing. However, one day we tried out each other's, and she thought the Chanel foundation was really oily, and the Armani sank into my pores and made my skin look terrible!

Marena

The problem with any luminous foundation is you nearly have to have perfect skin to begin with and most of us don't. I find these foundations look lovely on the cheeks and end up showing up everything on the T-zone, but it's relatively new and that's why they flog it so hard. Giorgio Armani has wonderful foundations. The Matte Silk foundation is for combination skin and I love it and it blends really well and you can layer it depending on the coverage you need. The Hydra Glow has an SPF in it and it's great for dry skin.

LMC

I love Giorgio Armani Luminous Silk in 5.5, and also MAC Full Coverage in NC35 goes on really nice with the MAC stipple brush which I could not live without – it's amazing! I also like Estée Lauder Double Wear, but it's too heavy for daytime, fab at night though.

9. Bargaintastic: Rimmel Renew and Lift

Rimmel has been surprising me all over the shop recently. Rimmel has been releasing some good products like Renew and Lift Foundation. It's great for more mature skin types, as it contains conditioning peptides and ceramides as well as SPF15. Medium coverage at a great price.

10. Piggy Bank Perfect: Maybelline Dream Matte Mousse

Providing you moisturise well beforehand, Maybelline's Dream Matte Mousse is a great budget buy. Easy to apply, the coverage is buildable, so if you like it sheer, just use a little; if you like move coverage, then lash on the whole pot. Well, not the whole pot, but you know what I mean. Young skin will love this foundation.

AISLING'S PICK: MAC Studio Fix Fluid with SPF 15

And the one I use? MAC Studio Fix Fluid with SPF 15 is the best foundation I have ever used. It's lovely and moisturising for dry skins, plus it gives great coverage and it comes in a brilliant range of shades.

CELEBRITY BEAUTY SECRETS: Bertie Ahern

Bertie is a practised hand at foundation. And no matter what you felt about his politics, he transformed himself from a grubby anorak-wearing backbencher into a Taoiseach who understood how important make-up is. He spent a lot – well, he did think he was worth it. The rumour mill has it that he used Armani foundations and that's a choice that many make-up artists would approve of. Our current politicians could do with a bit of this savvy. So lads, my advice is to hit the make-up counters and get one of the nice ladies there to cast her professional eye over you.

PRODUCTS OF YORE: Max Factor Pan Stick

Remember this awful, gloopy stuff? I'm not a fan, I'm afraid. Shiny, greasy and with far more coverage than

SJP's Mole
MAC Studio Fix compact foundation. I've been wearing it for yeeeeeaaaars. The compact is great because it takes you 10 seconds to bang it on and then you don't have to worry about it at all. It's great when you're in a sweaty nightclub, for example, as it's long lasting and pretty matte. Like all compacts, you can put it on as lightly or as thickly as you like depending on how much coverage you want. Also, if you do need any touch-ups, it's a quick flick out of the handbag and patpatpat on your nose and that's it!

Beautygeek

I know loadsa people have bad memories of this as it was a staple of teenage make-up bags around the country, but … Max Factor Pan Stick is Tony-the-Tiger ggrreeaat! It is creamy, long-lasting and looks pretty darn good on the skin! OK, so the colour range isn't that good, nor is the scent, and it isn't suitable for very oily skin, but I love it! I admit you need to touch up shine with a dab of powder every couple of hours, but it is a lovely product. I sometimes use it with the Dermalogica SPF drops dried onto my face and no moisturiser at all – reduces the shine, TRY IT !

Tori

I wear Clinique Supermoisture foundation and I find it's brilliant. I am prone to dry patches and this foundation saved my skin this winter.

anyone would ever need, it's really only meant for stars of stage and screen. As a teenager, Kirstie was accosted by a girl working in our local chemist who admired her. 'Yer make-up is lovely, young wan,' the sales assistant enthused. 'Oh, thanks!' replied the unsuspecting Kirstie, to be met with, 'Is it Panstick?' Home she came, in a rage of epic proportions. It most certainly was not Panstick. In fact, it was probably some horrible white make-up, layered over thick (and unnecessary) green concealer.

GET YER ROCKS OFF: MINERAL FOUNDATION

When Bare Escentuals developed their bareMinerals make-up – literally created from crushed-up rocks – a craze was born. 'So pure you can sleep in it', blazed the tagline. Heralded as the ultimate new beauty discovery, we don't agree at Beaut.ie – it's messy, there's a learning curve, the coverage can be very light and you'll have to shell out for some new brushes, too. But it's really taken off. As the interest in green cosmetics surged, a slew of copycat mineral brands hit the shelves, leaving everyone totally

confused, because of course all mineral make-up is not created equal. Cheap brands tend to be bulked up with talc, while the more expensive brands are, well, expensive.

So how does it work? The make-up is basically a powder that you buff onto skin using a specific tool, the Kabuki brush. Densely packed hair makes this the ultimate choice for minerals, and you won't get the same result with yer regular powder brush. Tip, swirl and tap is the method to use: tip a little into the lid of the pot, swirl the brush and then tap off the excess, then buff onto skin to your heart's content.

Mineral make-up is not for everyone, though. It may suit those of you who like a natural look during the day if you don't like the feel of liquid foundation clogging your pores. Watch out for brands that contain talc or bulking agents, as this means the product may settle into lines or cake. In general, dry skin doesn't fare particularly well with mineral make-up either, but of course cosmetic companies are eager to insist it suits everyone.

MontyC

I would highly recommend either Chanel Vitalumière (it comes in a fluid, a creme in a lovely little pot and creme compact) or YSL Perfect Touch foundations. I have pale, dry, sensitive skin and both of these foundations suit me down to the ground! At the moment though I'm using Chanel Mat Lumière and I love it too. But my fave is the Armani Hydra Glow.

Nicolina Moo

I adore mineral foundation, definitely one for greasy skin though. I only use moisturiser at night now, and then just whack the mineral on in the morning and my skin is amazing. Revlon's one is quite good, but my all-time favourite is from Lily Lolo.

miffyonline

I am another recent convert to Everyday Minerals after months of writing mineral make-up off as the 'next big thing of no real substance'. I have dry skin, lots of red undertones and find the make-up actually improves the texture of my skin.

Weewee

Jane Iredale's Liquid Minerals is the absolute best, there's nothing else like it on the market. It contains aloe and minerals and although it's very light, it offers complete coverage.

I reckon it's best suited to oily skin, and it might even be just the solution to stop your foundation sliding off your face by lunchtime. So go in and give it a try if this is a concern of yours, but remember the magic words – get samples before you buy!

So, while we're not madly keen on this sort of foundation, we have found three we think are worth the cash money.

Mineralogue

Just because it's not liquid doesn't mean you're going to magically get your shade right. If that's always your problem, check out Mineralogie's custom blending service. The exact shade for your skin tone can be magically mixed up, giving you a natural, tide-free finish. Hurrah!

Maybelline Mineral Power

Surprisingly good for a budget brand, Maybelline's Mineral Power Powder Foundation, in eight shades, is talc-free – and nice and budget-conscious, too. You can even get matching mineral shadow and blushes, too.

Kirstie

If you're new to minerals, a nice way to start is with eyeshadows or blush – Maybelline, L'Oréal and IsaDora do decent ranges at good prices. I'd tend to spend on the foundation, as that's going to be on a bigger area, so it's important it looks and feels right.

Prescriptives All Skins Mineral Makeup

This one's not a pure mineral, but all the better for it, we reckon. Prescriptives All Skins Mineral Makeup comes in 18 shades, provides good coverage that's great for day and, best of all, it won't cause the dreaded Gobi Desert effect on your fine lines and wrinkles.

Best of the Rest

Jane Iredale, bareMinerals, Lily Lolo and Everyday Minerals are recommended all the time too.

Ruth

Everyday Minerals make-up is deadly and it's cheaper than most of the other brands. You can order a free starter kit from them, you just pay postage and it works out at about $5: www.everdayminerals.com. Just don't buy the brushes though, they are rubbish. I use the MAC 182 kabuki. I have the Bobbi Brown kabuki too and that is also good.

Lin

bareMinerals is THE BUSINESS! I've had complements from friends since I started using it and the coverage is literally unbelievable – with just a little on the cute kabuki brush, you feel like you have nothing on your face yet all the imperfections are covered. Great for T-zone shine control as well – it doesn't eliminate shine (I think we all know that just ain't possible!) but certainly reduces it compared to liquid foundation and a quick swish of Mineral Veil at lunchtime and you're fresh as a daisy.

I LOVE the MAC 187 brush! I find it much better than the flat foundation brush that I can never get the hang of … always end up streaky. The 187 takes a bit of practice, but once you get used to it, it's easy and gives a lovely finish, and you can use it for powders too, so it's a good multi-purpose product. Make sure the sales assistant shows you exactly how to use it.

Step away from the sponge: but try the Beautyblender.

Sponges in general are a bit unhygienic and yuck, and they soak up product like nobody's business too. But the Beautyblender sponge, which comes complete with a special cleanser, is only deadly. Shaped to the planes of your face, it'll make you up in seconds – and we can forgive a bit of product-wastage for speed.

BRUSHES WITH BRILLIANCE

Right, it's confession time for me. I put foundation on with my fingers. There, I've said it.

I know lots of you turn your noses up at this and love to use brushes, so I've asked brush fiend Kirstie to help me out here. This is her advice.

Kirstie says, 'Not content with smearin' yer foundation on with your fingers? While there's no doubt it's what a lot of us do on a daily basis, if you want a pro finish, then a brush is the way to go. They do take a bit of getting used to – after all, you're pretty much painting your face, and you can end up with a not-so-flattering paint-effect finish, complete with streaks, if you're not careful. Perseverance and practice make perfect, I reckon. Foundation brushes are made from synthetic fibres, so they don't soak up product, which means they're really quite clever and economical. And sure, I like a bit of that.'

Make-up Artists' Choice

Everyone who uses MAC's 187 Duo Fibre Brush raves about it. It's a big circular brush that makes applying and blending liquid foundation a doddle. While it's a bit of an investment buy, if you want that airbrushed finish, this is the boyo for the job.

BRUSHES CAN GET STINKY

If you're a regular brush user, you'll find that your brushes can start to smell as ripe as the Irish rugby team's runners after a session with the All Blacks. So every couple of days – ideally after each use – work a little gentle shampoo into the bristles (baby shampoo is ideal), lather up with warm water and rinse until the water runs clear. Pat dry, reshape and leave somewhere warm to dry. Don't immerse your brush in water or you run the risk of the glue softening and your brush disintegrating.

Kirstie

Its soft, cuddly wee curves actually make it really, really easy to use when applying foundation. You truly do get a streak-free finish and you do use more product with the Beautyblender sponge than you would with fingers.

CONCEALER AND ILLUMINATOR

Concealer is a very useful thing to have tucked away in the make-up bag. Like foundation, it should never look obvious. No one should be able to pinpoint the presence of concealer: all they should know is that you look somehow brighter, more awake and that you've had years taken off you.

Let's face it, unless you're as fresh faced as a little daisy, you're going to have need of a concealer once in a while (or every day, in my case). And never have any nights out on the razz. And spend your days drinking pure water, eating broccoli and getting eight hours of sleep … Right so, that's settled. We all need a bit of help, eh?

There's nothing else that can so dramatically and instantly lift your complexion and make you look fresher. And younger – let's not forget that – up to five years younger. To hide spots and blemishes, though, make sure you don't use an illuminating product (like Touche Éclat), as it will actually draw more attention to them.

So when should you be putting it on? If you cover up all the dark circles and zits before you whack on the foundation, you'll probably find you don't need to use as much product – and that's a good thing, as it'll leave you with a nice natural-looking finish. But sure, it's up to you.

How to Apply Concealer

Apply with your fingers (the heat in your hands melts the product slightly and helps to work it in) and press or pat softly into skin *before* you put on your foundation. The place that most people really need concealer is in the eye sockets, which have a habit of remaining stubbornly black no matter how much sleep you've gotten. Just press some concealer into the corner of your eye by your nose and this will make a real difference to your face, instantly brightening the area. Don't fill in your entire under-eye area with concealer.

Not all concealers meet the job spec, so here's my pick of the best perfection-enhancers.

Jenknee
I use Laura Mercier Secret Camouflage on spots and Touche Éclat under the eyes.

Illuminating

Now ladies, Touche Éclat, as we've previously mentioned, is not a concealer. Rather, it's designed to add light and luminosity to dull, dark areas – like those eye bags you could carry the week's shopping home in. Pat it on there, and very definitely leave it off zits, boils and spots. You've been warned.

Natural Coverage

Bobbi Brown's Creamy Concealer is a wonder product that instantly lifts the eye area, hiding dark circles and all those signs that you're not quite as fresh-faced as you'd like to be. Bonus? You can use it to mask blemishes and spots too.

BUDGET BUY

You'd be hard pressed to find a better product than Barbara Daly for Tesco's concealer at such a supermarket-tastic price point. But this stuff is the business – creamy and imperfection-disguising, it's non-drying and doesn't cake either. Bravo! Don't forget to check out Aldi's fab Lacura Beauty Concealer Pen, too.

Trillian II

I use the No. 7 version of Touche Éclat – I find it better than the real thing. Benefit's Boi-ing is good, but I agree with the caking thing – it looks good for an hour, but then makes me look like I'm 10 years older than I am.

AISLING'S PICK:
Benefit Realness of Concealness

I carry Benefit's Realness of Concealness around with me all the time. It's a perfect little box of tricks for anyone looking to do a bit of complexion enhancing. Miniature versions of Benefit's best-selling Lemon-Aid, Boi-ing, Ooh La Lift, Lip Plump and High Beam make this fake-it kit a must-have.

Boozy Floozy

I got the Barbara Daly for Tesco one on someone's recommendation here and it's great. Like war paint! I use it under my eyes but the girl beside me in work told me I looked tired Monday and Tuesday so am afraid I used too much and had a weird all one-tone ghostly face!

dancingqueen

MAC Studio Finish is excellent, great coverage and staying power. Much too heavy for under your eyes, though. Really covers scars or spots or red marks.

GracieBear

Just whacked on some Bare Escentuals Well Rested Eye Brightener. Picked it up during summer in the States. Looks very good actually, though I don't know how it will last during the day. Looks better than Benefit Erase Paste.

THE REVERSE PANDA

The reverse wha? This happens when you apply a thick layer of illuminator or concealer in a solid ring below the eyes. The effect? That of a panda's eyes in negative. Lovely, eh?

PRODUCT OF YORE:
No. 7 Colour Calming Make-up Base

We think they've done a number on this because it sure as hell looks a lot nicer now. In days of yore, we lashed this on under our snow-white foundation to combat any potential rosiness. We didn't have high colour then, and we don't have it now – but back then, we thought we were the bee's knees. Oh, the shame.

Tish

I use Benefit's Boi-ing and find it really good. I also love the Clarins pen one – can't remember the name of it. Works miracles! And I always used to put it on after foundation until I read the Bobbi Brown tips on beaut.ie, and it makes such a huge difference putting it on before foundation – way better.

THE PRIME OF YOUR LIFE

Primers can be fantastic for giving make-up a smooth, professional-looking finish and making sure they stay put. If you have very sebum-prone skin, primers or mattifying moisturisers applied first can help. Be wary of using primer every day – many contain silicones, and they block pores and don't allow skin to breathe very well, so saving them for special occasions is best. Here's another clever way to use your primer: if you look for one with a built-in SPF, then you're adding an extra level of protection against harmful UV rays too.

AISLING'S PICK:
Smashbox Photo Finish Foundation Primer

I love, love, love Photo Finish Foundation Primer from Smashbox. It's got a silky texture that glides across skin, filling in pores and uneven skintone. Smooth your foundation over the top and be amazed at how fabilis you look. It's like airbrushing in a bottle! Don't use every day as it can clog your pores – save for special occasions!

smashbox

PHOTO FINISH

FOUNDATION PRIMER
UNIFICATEUR DE TEINT

.93 Fl.Oz.℮ 27.5ml

Jill
Hmm, they may do the same thing, but Givenchy Perfect Again! looks like it has slightly more sympathetic concealing colours. I went through a phase in my late teens where I was convinced I had the rosiest clown cheeks in the world that could only be dampened by a tube of No. 7 green stuff. I must have looked sick all that year!

Zita

I totally rate Benefit's Dr. Feelgood for keeping foundation looking 'just applied' for longer. I have combination skin and find that using a tag team of a good primer before applying liquid foundation and Dr. Feelgood after applying makes a huge difference in how long my foundation remains looking good.

Seal

A light spray of hairspray is excellent for setting make-up too! Spray far away from your face (and keep your eyes closed!). People think I'm silly when I recommend this, but artists do it to set chalk drawings and it works!

MontyC

Dior and Chanel do gorgeous translucent powders.

Great Sun Protection

Get a two-in-one effect with MAC's clever Prep + Prime Face Protect primer. With a whopping SPF50, you'll be shielded from the sun, plus the priming element gives your foundation a good way to cling to your skin, helping it to last longer.

DOUBLE TAKE: HAIRSPRAY

Bet you never knew that beauty-standard hairspray can be used for something other than setting your 'do into rock-hard formation. Yup, you can use it to set your make-up too – if you're brave enough.

POWDER UP

Now this is a tough one too. Jesus, nothing in this chapter is easy, is it? Choose the wrong powder and you can wind up with a face that looks as though it belongs in a morgue: flat, white and with powder settling into every fine line. Fine if you're going for the Goth look of the mid-Eighties. Not so great if you want to look like a normal soul.

But powder is an essential part of finishing off your foundation, helping to set it in place and keep it there for the day, so it's really worth getting it right.

Rule number one: less is more. Seriously, just wave the stuff at your face. Don't be tempted to load up either a puff or brush with a ton of it, because this is where it'll all start to go horribly wrong.

Rule number two: use a translucent powder. Coloured versions will affect how your foundation looks, and there's no point in choosing an exact match only to ruin it all at the finishing stage.

For application, brushes are best, as puffs have a tendency to smear liquid foundation. Gently swirl your brush into loose or pressed powder, tap off any excess, and with feather-light movements, dust over the face. If your skin has a tendency to dryness, just lightly dust the T-zone. If your skin is a bit more generous in the sebum department, then give your whole face a light dusting.

Kirstie
The Laura Mercier Mineral Finishing Powder is superb. I'm at the end of my jar though, and bereft!

Monika
Usually it's talc in the powder that's drying. You could try Lucidity by Estée Lauder. Gives a lovely finish and is talc free.

Powder Picks

Laura Mercier's Mineral Finishing Powder is the bomb for setting fluid and cream foundations. Light as air, bag the translucent shade to finish your make-up without adding unwanted colour.

Bit on the expensive side? You could do worse than check out Rimmel's powder offerings. Their Silky Loose Face Powder is translucent and pocket friendly.

11

Cheeky Girls

...WE'VE GOT BLUSHER, BRONZER, HIGHLIGHTERS, CHEEK STAINS, ILLUMINATORS...

Once upon a time, there was blusher, pure and simple. It was either cream or powder and all you had to worry about was where to put it. Now we've got blusher, bronzer, highlighters, cheek stains, illuminators … What are they all for? And where in the name of jaysus do we put them?

BRONZER

Now this can be a tricky one for us Irishers. We tend to go a bit mad with the aul' bronzer, slapping it on willy nilly under the misguided impression that we're giving ourselves a 'healthy glow', when in fact all we're doing is making ourselves look fluorescent and frightening to small children.

The problem here is that many bronzers are, well, just too bronze for us. Just like a lot of fake tans, the shade can be primarily formulated for other, more sallow-skinned races, so we have to be very careful. But when it all comes together and works, bronzer is a thing of joy and beauty. It can pick up your whole complexion and make you look only fabilis. Try one of these bronzers, following the essential Lovely Girls rule, of course – try before you buy. If you don't recognise yourself in mirrors or Mammy spits out her tea in surprise when she sees you, you've probably chosen too dark a shade.

Apply bronzer lightly wherever the sun would kiss you naturally: the tops of your cheeks, your chin, your nose and your forehead. Remember to take it up the sides of your face too, to shape and contour. If you're new to this bronzing business, try a baked bronzer. Lighter in formulation and not so colour saturated, they're particularly good for very pale lassies.

THE **BEAUT.IE** GUIDE TO GORGEOUS

Natural Glow

I've got nothing but glowing recommendations for NARS Laguna – it's a soft shade that won't make you look as though you've got dirt on your face instead of bronzer.

Beginner's Bronzer

Check out Urban Decay's Baked Bronzer if you're a wee bit scared of turning yourself into a tangoed woman. This is light and lovely and brilliant for adding a hint of a sun-kissed shimmer to super-pale skin.

Everyone Loves Guerlain

Guerlain Terracotta Light Sheer Bronzing Powder wins hands down for Irish skin. Subtle tones, gorgeous texture and a luxury feel, this is the one to go for if you want a look that's understated and yet manages to bestow a great glow.

Brilliant Budget Buy

Rimmel Sun Shimmer Bronzing Compact Powder is hard to beat on price and effectiveness. Just use a light hand with it, as some shades can be little too dark for pale skins.

Zinnie

The bronzer I find most natural, not shiny, but not talc(y) either is NARS Laguna – love, love, love this bronzer. I also use it as a base on my eyes sometimes, goes great with smokey greys/purples.

Lynnie

There are two shades of the Guerlain Bronzer Light: 01 for blondes, which has pinker tones, and 02 for brunettes, which has more peach tones. And there is a lovely, subtle shimmer to it which sounds like what you're after, it's nowhere near as gaudy as the likes of Lancôme Star Bronzer, which always made me feel like a disco ball.

MontyC

Terracotta 10 is the best bronzer around. I have very fair skin (and blonde hair) and the Guerlain bronzers are the only ones that look natural on me! They 'warm' me up without making me look orange! Pure genius.

BRONZING COMPACTS AND BRUSHES

Just to make matters a little more confusing, blushers and bronzers can also come in mosaic or striped compacts and in pre-loaded brushes. This is sheer genius, so embrace it. The colour won't look one-dimensional because as your brush sweeps across the palette, it picks up all the different complementary shades – meaning you won't end up with flat tiger stripes on your cheeks. As an added bonus, these mosaics often contain highlighters (look out for the little white squares) so one palette does more than one job at once. I, for one, totally love that.

Ladyelvis

I have started using Revlon Bronzer in 02 – gorgeous colour and lasts all day. Comparable to Dior I think!

If you're not a fan of shimmer during the day, then go for a matte palette. Just tell them at the make-up counter exactly what look you want to create, and obviously avoid anything called 'Shimmer Brick' or similar.

Brush Bronzer: Lancôme StarBronzer Magic Brush

Ever since I first bought Lancôme StarBronzer Magic Brush on the plane on the way back from Spain many moons ago, this has been a make-up bag staple and has been replaced time and time again. St. Tropez have one of these fellas too, and while there are far better bronzers out there, these are really handy for the handbag, and the click-and-apply system means I always have one with me.

Duo Powder: Paul & Joe Face Color Powder

Paul & Joe Face Color Powders come in tons of shades and colourways. Choose from bronzer and a highlighter in one, or a blusher and bronzer. Oh, I love these dual-purpose cosmetics, and like all their make-up, this one from cult brand Paul & Joe looks so pretty too. And remember, dressing table appeal is a big part of any cosmetic's desirability.

NIGHT-TIME SHIMMER AND SHINE

Bobbi Brown Shimmer Brick takes the prize. A thing of beauty is a joy forever, and the Shimmer Brick is gorgeous. The striped tones of this blusher/bronzer/highlighter compact make it a cinch to get gorgeous colour with one sweep of a blusher brush. Pick from pink, copper or bronzy shades.

AISLING'S PICK: Smashbox Fusion Soft Lights

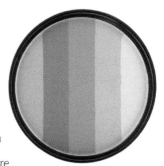

Smashbox Fusion Soft Lights are a winner for me. Fab pinks, peaches and highlighter blend together and are perfect for that blusher brush soft-sweep that flatters and enhances. Don't, for the love of god, drop it or carry it around in your make-up bag though – this will live up to its name and smash – everywhere.

TOP TIPS FOR BLUSHER

Lots of people wonder why they need blusher at all. Well, I'll tell you why – what foundation covers up, blusher puts back in, but where you want it. And that's the genius of blush, but remember – less is more. Make no mistake, you *will* look like a painted hoor if you put too much on. Be judicious in your application – start off with a light dusting, tapping the brush to remove excess powder before applying it to your face. Remember, you can always apply more if needs be.

For god's sake, use a decent blusher brush. Don't use the little yoke that came with the blusher. This is as bad as applying eyeshadow with the little sponge applicators that come in compacts. You will only have yourself to blame if you end up with pink stripes on your face.

Suck in your cheeks and apply the blush to the bit of your cheek (the apple) above the hollow. Take it up the side of your face towards your ears. Blend it in really well. This is an absolutely great way to frame the face and make you look very sculpted and sexy. If you're new to blusher, use powder – it's easier to manage than cream.

Great Blush Picks
Benefit Dandelion

Benefit Dandelion is soft, sweet, adorable. It's like My First Blusher. Absolutely ideal for Irish skin and daytime wear, this little box of matte pink blusher can be worn by just about anyone. It creates a pretty-looking natural colour. I love it – and so do most of you, judging by the comments we receive regularly about it.

Cream Blush: Clinique Blushwear

Avoid cream blushers if you've a lot of open pores on your cheeks, as the formulation will highlight them. But they're so versatile and easy to use – just remember to apply over foundation and before powder. I love Clinique Blushwear Cream Stick in Shy Blush, which is subtle and lovely for a day in the office.

FAKE AN ORGASM

So called because it fakes the flush granted by an, er, orgasm, the NARS hero blusher is absolutely perfect for Irish skin. It's loved by millions – the blusher, I mean. Check out Super Orgasm too for a shot of sparkle. Well worth the spend.

Twinkletoes
Blusher is either NARS Orgasm, Benefit Dandelion or a Pout one (sadly no longer available when this runs out). Orgasm is my fave, though Dandelion is good for a more natural everyday flush.

Chica
My fave blushers are MAC Blushcreme in Blossoming and Sweet William (I love cream blushers!) or a cheapy – Boots 17 Blush in Plum Puff.

Lin
Rimmel Mono Blush in Santa Rose – great for a natural rosy look for fair-skinned ladies!

Revlon Matte Powder Blush

Not everyone wants shimmery cheeks, especially for daywear. So that's why we were so pleased to find out about Revlon's matte blushers. Great prices, and they come in pretty shades.

WORK OF SATAN: Orange Bronzer

Orange bronzer. Come on, girls – stop this evil now. Give yourself a good hard look in the mirror and make sure you've not been tangoed. Bronzer should not cover your whole face, it should just highlight and warm you up a bit. You know you're gorgeous – just don't cover it up with a heavy layer of Jaffa-coloured powder.

Twinkletoes

Highlighter is Benefit High Beam or MAC Strobe Cream. I just use it on my cheekbones/temples.

Benefit High Beam

Benefit makes gorgeous highlighters and their best-selling High Beam is the one to have in your make-up bag. Dot it onto brow and cheekbones, lightly blend and you'll look glowy and gorgeous.

ILLUMINATORS AND HIGHLIGHTERS

These both work in similar ways, bouncing light off the face and thus increasing radiance. They work incredibly well to shape the face and create a youthful glow. Whether they're cream, powder or liquid, you use them at the top of your cheekbones, brow bone or anywhere you want to draw attention to.

That dewy glow is something we'd all like to have. Like anything else, if you don't have it naturally, simply fake it. But a little note, if you please: these are best kept for night, and make sure you apply sparingly, with a decent contouring brush.

MAC Strobe Cream

MAC highlighters are a thing of joy and Strobe Cream is loved by make-up artists – and by us. It's a white, shimmering cream you can use to highlight skin with, but a wee word of warning: this stuff is high-octane, so only a very little is needed.

Top Tip: If you don't want to spend on a dedicated highlighter, you can also use a gold or silver shimmer shadow, like one of Barry M's Dazzle Dusts or MAC's pigments. Just use a light hand!

Ladyelvis
Kevyn Aucoin highlighter in Champagne is AMAZING at night!

Dellie
I use a highlighter from the Barbara Daly range at Tesco and it's fab!

Brownbella
I have Benefit's High Beam, which is great for any time of year and any time of night or day. And I've Mr. Frosty, which is a white shimmer pencil, great for highlighting under the brow, very sexy with smokey eyes.

CELEBRITY MAKEOVER

Ah, Bosco. Even as a child, I hated you, with your irritating high-pitched shriek and your shrill cries. Your overexcited antics wrecked my after-school relaxation of squash and rich teas, and now as an adult I have come to despise you for another reason: your blusher. In fact, your whole 'look' in general. I mean, did no one ever tell you that red dreads made out of wool are a style no-no? *Uafásach* is right.

Christine

Seeing as he's a redhead, he should go for Orgasm from NARS or Portofino for a healthy summer glow. Then again, he really shouldn't be wearing make-up – and there was me thinking that Shirley Templebar was the first male on TV to wear 'obvious' make-up!

Jenknee

Bosco must be in his 40s now, so his voice would have broken. He should get rid of the stripy green smock and head into Louis Copeland for a nice tin of fruit. I would cut his red dreads and give him a spiky head of hair and some eyebrows.

You ensured that you would go down in history as the worst crisis ever suffered by the RTÉ make-up department – apart from Pat Kenny's orange foundation, that is. It's no wonder that poor Sharon Ní Bheoláin chooses to do her own make-up.

How can we make over Bosco? He'll thank us for it. Assuming he's still alive, that is. Well Bosco, I've thought long and hard about this one and it just seems as though you should calm things down. Start afresh, as it were. A good hairdresser will tone down the frantic colour of your wool and add nice caramel and toffee tones. Next, a trip to the beautician's, where your wooden features can be refreshed with linseed oil.

Finally, the make-up. Your red blusher will be replaced with the much more subtle pinky glow of Benefit Dandelion, easy to wear and flattering to just about everyone. Now you can go to sleep easy in your box.

TEDDY BOBBS TELLS US HOW TO FIX BROKEN MAKE-UP

Now girrrls, yis needen't be weeping when ye open that compact to find the powder inside is smashed to smithereens. There's no need to be shelling out for another one. Here are a couple of things to be trying.

STEP ONE Put a tissue over the top of the whole mess and press it down firmly. Repeat this a few times and you might find it's useable again. Close the lid and keep the tissue on top. But you'll always have to treat it with a bit of the auld TLC and you can't be carrying it around.

STEP TWO Pop down to the chemist and get some surgical spirit. Mix a tiny bit of it in with the smashed powder and leave it in a warm place to dry (somewhere like the hot press is A-OK). You can't be doing this with a palette, though, unless you want everything to turn the colour of used Play-Doh.

marquise

I've repaired broken eyeshadows with surgical spirits and they are as good as new! The only thing is the stench from the surgical spirits, so you have to leave the fixed eyeshadow to air out for a few days!

Larianne

I think it depends on the type – matte/creme eyeshadows tend not to break, but shadows which have more glitter/sparkle in them tend to break – maybe due to the fact that the powder isn't solid due to different elements in them. It's always the lovely glittery ones!

12

Bat for Lashes

There must be no other small part of our anatomy that has so much time, money and energy spent on it...

Okay, I know they're teeny tiny areas, but they're highly important ones. So I make my case to you, members of the jury: brows and lashes deserve their own section. Why? Unless you're from a place where the monobrow is considered the height of fashion and attractiveness, i.e. nowhere, you'll be glad of this section.

While I was writing this book, they burst out of every chapter I slotted them into, wailing, 'We don't belong here! We need our own section.' At a loss to know what to do with them, I granted their request. They were making other chapters too huge and unwieldy anyway, causing me sleepless nights and dreams filled with cartoon villains brandishing eyelash curlers and other gruesome implements.

And my final argument: they frame the windows of the soul. I rest my case.

LOVELY LASHES

There must be no other small part of our anatomy that has so much time, money and energy spent on it. Any discussion on Beaut.ie about lashes provokes so much interest, it's amazing. Lashes to make Bambi jealous are what we're all after, frankly. There's no end of things you can be doing with the lashes. And guess what – I've done most of them. And if I haven't, you can be sure one of the Beaut.ies has!

EYELASH CURLERS

It's often been said these yokes look like implements of medieval torture, but they work fantastically well. I'm not saying anything new here when I tell you that the few seconds they add to your beauty routine is well worth it. They'll open up your eyes and make you look wide awake – and, of course, more gorgeous.

If you want to give yourself really curly lashes, curl your lashes and then use a waterproof lengthening mascara. When the waterproof mascara has dried, apply a lengthening mascara, but only to the tips of the lashes. The waterproof mascara sets the curl and the second coat of mascara makes the tips of the lashes visible.

Top Tip: For the love of god, remember to use your eyelash curlers *before* mascara, never after. Especially if you're using heated ones, otherwise you'll just bake the mascara onto your lashes.

Eyelash Perming

You'll have to go to a salon to get this done. Don't even think of attempting it at home, as perming solution so near the eyes is a disaster waiting to happen.

Perming lotion will be applied to your lashes after the therapist has used a little roller and water-soluble glue to separate and roll eyelashes. It's left on for a short time (usually about 15 minutes) and then neutraliser is applied – just like a regular perm.

sue
I don't have a heated eyelash curler but I can recommended holding your hairdryer on your own curlers before you use them, works a treat!

Dolly
I heat my normal eyelash curler with the hairdryer and then curl my lashes, it works much better than heated curlers. Make sure, though, to test the heat of it on your hand first, burnt eyelids are not pretty.

Yeah roigh!
I've got a Blinc heated eyelash curler and it works! Except you DO have to hold it quite close to the eyelid for a good few seconds and it feels VERY hot… so potential for a scalded eyelid methinks. But deffo better than ye olde clamping version.

Lynnie

They use different size rollers depending on the length of your own lashes and the kind of effect you want to achieve. So for a really tight, Barbie curl or for someone with short eyelashes, they should use a teeny roller to get a good effect. Lots of Asian girls with particularly short lashes rave about it.

Ava

I had my make-up done at the Stila counter in BT's and the make-up artist curled my lashes first at the root and then again halfway along the lash and the results were amazing! I never, ever used to bother curling my lashes (they are actually very long), but since then I've been doing it every day and I've been asked repeatedly if I'm wearing false lashes!

This takes the whole concept of eyelash curling to an extreme. I've never had it done, and quite frankly I'm not too keen on the whole idea, but it's becoming more popular and some of you seem to love it. If you've got short lashes, it seems to be worthwhile, but if you've got naturally long lashes, I wouldn't bother. Stick with the old-fashioned curlers.

FeeFee

I got this done a year ago and found it great for the first week or two but a big downside was that as it was growing out individual lashes were losing their curl. When I put on mascara it looked funny, as some lashes were very curled and some were back to normal. Curling manually did help but only for an hour or two!

FALSE EYELASHES

If you want to bat your eyes and cause a draught in a room, then falsies are yer only man. They are notoriously difficult to put on, though, and can be really fiddly. Shu Uemura, MAC, Essence and Eylure all do good ones, at varying prices. If you're new to falsies, go for individual ones and work up from there. A few strategically placed individual lashes can have a striking effect (try concentrating on the outer corner of your eye) and you may not want to go for a full strip. If you really want to bling it up, go for falsies with feathers or rhinestones.

Individual Lashes

If you're only going to use one or two lashes to build up a sparse lash-line or add a flirty kick to the corner of your eyes, then Eylure's Individual Lashes are fab – you get tons of different lengths in the pack, so they'll last for ages.

Statement Lashes

Check out Make Up For Ever for feather- and jewel-encrusted creations that wouldn't be out of place at a haute couture fashion show. Brilliant for special occasions and fancy dress parties, if you're careful with application and removal, you'll get up to three wears from each pair.

Eyelash Extensions

If you've got short, sparse lashes, then eyelash extensions will make a difference to you. If your lashes are naturally long, don't bother – no one will notice the difference. They look really natural, so don't confuse them with the full-on look of false eyelashes.

This is how the magic happens. The therapist will place a soft pad over your lower lashes so that the top and bottom eyelashes don't stick together when the glue is applied. Then you close your eyes for the time of the treatment. The extensions are glued onto your natural lashes. It's a painstaking process.

Lynnie
I usually get one eye on perfectly and then the other goes totally arseways on me. I did manage to get a pair on exactly right once and they were gorgeous so I keep at it like an eejit. I'm grand with individuals 'cos I just lash them in there with a tweezers and a prayer, but I always feck up full strips, generally attaching one end to my lashes, and the other to body parts including, variously, nose, cheeks and eyelids.

Sarah
At the moment I'm loving the lashes from Dianne Brill in Clerys. They come in a cute little hatbox with three different sets, and they're all reusable.

letsmakeup
Have to say gals, I can't beat the Essence ones, they're just fab.

Twinkletoes

It really does get addictive! I loved mine, but after a few fills I had to wean myself off because it's expensive enough. Mine lasted about three to four weeks before needing a top-up, that was with no mascara on them. Your eyes look so crap afterwards though when you're used to having the extensions!

Each extension is applied separately and dried with a little puff of air. Not painstaking for you, of course. Nope, no work is required from you – just lie on the therapy couch and drift off.

The extensions can last for the lifetime of the eyelash. Each person has a different lash lifecycle, but generally speaking, you can expect to get weeks or even months out of this treatment. You have to take special care of the extensions, though – use a water-soluble mascara and remover. Ask your therapist for details about the aftercare for your lashes.

You can go back and get a top-up treatment after a couple of weeks where they will give you even more lashes. This should cost about half the price of the initial treatment, but be warned – just like gel nails, this is an addictive treatment (though not as harmful) with the potential to become budget-busting if you let it!

MOST WANTED: MASCARA

The most saturated part of the cosmetics market, not a week seems to go by without another new mascara hitting the shops. You want wild claims? You want an over-hyped product on heavy advertising rotation? You want a thousand shades of black? You got it!

But how the heck do you actually know which ones are great, which ones are OK and which ones are downright crap? You ask people who've tried them, that's how.

We've tried 'em all at Beaut.ie and then some, and we've come to the conclusion that although some of the luxe brands are fantastic and well worth the euro, some of the cheaper ones are just as effective. Mascara technology (just bear with me here) has advanced so quickly in a cut-throat market that there's no reason not to try out the less-expensive brands. Snobbery should have no place in a make-up bag. As with all beauty products, what's good and what works should always be given priority.

Top Tip: when you're applying mascara, place the wand at the root of the lashes and then zig-zag it back out to the tips – you'll get great coverage with minimal clumps. And don't forget the lashes at the outer corner of the eyes. Use the mascara that's gathered at the top of the tube and coat them well – you'll look immediately wider eyed and super-flirty.

THE BEAUT.IE TOP 10 MASCARAS

Best Mascara Brand

Hands down, it has to be Lancôme. Virtually all of their mascaras are really good and there are products to volumise, lengthen and curl. But the two I'd single out for particular praise are Oscillation, a motorised wonder that's a whizz (geddit?) at volumising lashes, and Virtuose, brilliant for dramatic eyes.

lips & lashes
Lancôme Virtouse is just a brilliant product, but then I always loved the Lancôme mascaras, I find them the best for me. But I also love the Bourjois Pump Up the Volume when I am stuck or the funds are low.

Sar
I use the Virtuose as well and find that the usually brilliant Bi-Facial (which can nearly get eye make-up off in one swipe) has a bit of a struggle with it. I think Lancôme does do the best mascaras though, especially lengthening ones.

AISLING'S PICK:
Bobbi Brown Everything Mascara

A noted beauty writer told us that this was as black as priest's socks, and she was right – Bobbi Brown's Everything Mascara is super-black and great for day. I love it.

Lancôme Oscillation

Motorised mascaras pioneered by Estée Lauder and Lancôme, we love the Lancôme version the very best. Oscillation thickly buzzes product onto lashes, and its vibrating action simultaneously works to dispel clumps. They sound gimmicky – they *are* gimmicky. But they do work!

DiorShow Mascara

Take a bow, DiorShow Mascara. A big, bumptious wand coats lashes brilliantly, adding unprecedented volume. You'll be amazed – and as it's waterproof, it won't budge until you come at it with the make-up remover.

Chanel Inimitable

Bee
Gotta say, for a daytime mascara, I find the Inimitable hard to beat. I have the Lancôme Virtuose and like it, but find it so difficult to get off. It's Inimitable all the way for me.

With its sleek black packaging and classy double-C logo, Chanel's Inimitable is bleedin' brilliant. Some may not love the wand, but I find it gets down tight into the lashline and zips out fabilisly, giving you amazing, defined eyes.

Max Factor Masterpiece

Hard to beat for those who don't want to splash out on a department store brand, Max Factor's Masterpiece range is brilliant. Great definition, nice brushes and slinky packaging make these boyos really good buys.

Rimmel Magnif'eyes

Magnif'eyes by Rimmel exceeds all expectations based on the price point. It coats well, really builds the lashes and provides a dramatic, noticeable finish.

Maybelline Lash Stilleto

With packaging that's shaped like a fancy heel, well, we were already sold. This mascara lengthens really well, and it's a great price too.

Clinique Lash Power

If you want to apply mascara at 7 a.m. and have it look the same come 7 p.m., then try Clinique's Lash Power Mascara. With a longwearing formula, it doesn't budge until you want it to.

BAD BEHAVIOUR: MOST HATED MASCARA ISSUES

- **Clumping:** We can put up with a lot of bad behaviour from our mascara, but it seems as though the one thing we can't tolerate is clumping. If it clumps and gunks and sticks your eyelashes together, it defeats the purpose of a mascara, which is obviously to lengthen and darken and create more fantastic lashes. If it's clumping, it ain't doing that.

- **Eye irritation:** This is a bad one. Seemingly harmless brands may irritate your eyes all too easily and you will spend the whole day feeling as though needles are poking you in the eyeball. Go for a super gentle brand like Almay if this happens to you with almost every mascara.

- **Flaking down face:** Not a good look. Oh, how many mascaras have dashed my hopes by going on perfectly only to create an alluring panda-eyed effect a few hours later. Sign of crapness. Get rid of it.

- **Drying up too quickly:** *So* annoying. If it does this and you're in utter need of mascara, you can try putting it on the radiator to try and de-gunk it. But be warned that this is a cry for help from mascara and it's really telling you that it's old and tired and probably full of bacteria and needs to lie down in a nice quiet bin. Get rid of it pronto.

- **Awkward brush:** Very personal choice, this one. Some people (me included) hate the comb-style brush with its uncanny ability to stab you in the eye. Others love it but hate big bog-brush-type brushes. It's simply up to you.

Tish
Felt like a mini person using a giant's mascara when I started using Benefit BADgal first, but now I feel like a giant using anything else … love the giant brush!

cailín
Bought the L'Oréal Telescopic Clean mascara last week, it really is worth the money, fab lashes, long, clean and defined.

Mascara Primer

I was converted to mascara primer when I met up with a couple of Smashbox make-up artists to have a sneaky peek at their new make-up collection. I noticed straight away that one of them had the most fantastic eyelashes and of course I had to ask her what manner of false eyelashes/extensions they were. They were incredible, full on and long, long, long. Wherever she got them, I wanted some.

They were her natural lashes, though, and she put it all down to Smashbox Eyelash Primer. It coats lashes, making them full and thick, and mascara glides on smoothly over it.

You know those double-wanded lash-building mascaras with the white and black wands? The white side is basically a primer. Primer is a bodybuilding treatment for lashes – if you want to pump up the volume of even the most weedy of lashes, you should try a primer.

Top Tip: Primer works really well with cheaper mascara. This was a discovery we made at one of our Beaut.ie Brunches. Eyelash primer (especially the Smashbox primer) is brilliant, we agreed. But one thing we'd all found: it doesn't work as well with expensive mascaras. It works really well with Max Factor, Rimmel and Maybelline mascaras, plumping lashes and making them appear longer. Expensive mascaras seem to be better on their own. Strange, but true.

gingersnap

Girls, I have to let you into a big beauty secret of mine! I get lots of compliments for my eyelashes, even from beauty consultants in Brown Thomas – and my secret is … Shiseido Mascara Base! It's absolutely fabulous.

Kyia

I use the Smashbox primer with Maybelline Great Lash Blackest Black Mascara and it's fantastic, I love it, my eyelashes are so long and plump with it (have got so many comments on it). Would never go back to using mascara without using this primer.

ams

I own the Shiseido primer and I found it was crap with my Lancôme mascaras (Virtouse and Hypnôse). However, with my L'Oréal Telescopic it is fantastic – it's a really good mascara on its own, but with the primer it gives the false lashes look.

Greenofeye

I love coloured mascara … the brighter the better. A nice way of making my eyes pop with very little work.

Lynnie

I've a soft spot for navy/dark blue mascaras I have to say; find them great for taking the mixomatosis-looking edge off my 'morning after the night before' eyes!

Gingerrama

I once had my lashes tinted a blue-black. Amazing. Whites of eyes looked whiter. Might even have made my yellow teeth look whiter too. That might be wishful thinking (mind you, it's the yellow of very solid enamel, so should last a while, touch wood). And these really dark but not black shades do magical things on subtly changing your eye colour. Try it…

COLOURED MASCARA

Coloured mascara has come a long way since you were a teenager, and now comes in all sorts of sophisti-cat colours. Particularly flattering are the more natural-looking shades of the colour wheel, so look for jewel shades and try to avoid neons at all costs. Unless, of course, you're heading to a fancy dress party.

Great Jewel Shades

Step forward, Yves Saint Laurent Luxurious Mascara. Check out their flattering range of navy, violet and burgundy colours. And such pretty gold packaging too! Barry M is also great for cheap coloured mascaras.

BEAUTY MYTH: TRIMMING EYELASHES MAKES THEM LONGER

Now we all know about trimming our eyebrows into shape, but trimming or plucking eyelashes? Surely not! Sounding as barbaric as ducking possible witches in the village pond, this practice nevertheless still exists.

My attention was first drawn to the carry-on of trimming eyelashes when someone emailed me to find out if it makes them grow longer and curl upwards. Upon investigation, it seemed that a lot of people vividly remembered a family member trimming their eyelashes when they were a baby or toddler. This would be a vivid memory, all right. If anyone had approached me while I was strapped into my pram waving a nail scissors in front of my eyes, I don't think I could ever forget it either.

Now these same people think their Bambi-length lashes are down to this bout of madness, so I'm here to dispel this myth. Sorry people, but in the same way that trimming your hair won't encourage it to grow (it will make it appear healthier and fuller though), trimming your eyelashes can't possibly make them grow longer. All hair is basically programmed by the hair follicle to grow to a certain length and have a certain lifespan. What you do after this is not going to make a blind bit of difference.

Scissors and eyelashes: never the twain should meet. And as for plucking your eyelashes? That's got a medical name and if you are tempted to do it, it's time to seek help. My advice: buy a good mascara. That will do wonders for you altogether.

BROWS

This tremendously expressive part of our anatomy can be the cause of much angst. Every season, we're told that such and such a shape is 'so in' and 'so now'. It's true that you can easily date a photograph just by looking at eyebrows. Forget carbon dating – this method is far more accurate. Within seconds, future generations will instantly know if they're looking at a picture of the 1920s (think Greta Garbo) or the 1980s (think Brooke Shields). A mere sixty years, but eyebrow fashion paints an instant picture. Full and bushy in the Eighties, plucked to high heaven in the Twenties.

So within reason, find the shape that suits you. Don't slavishly follow fashion. If you like your brows to have an arch but the pictures in the magazines all say this season's look is straight – so what? Go with what suits the shape of your face.

And should you match your collar to your cuffs? If you've dyed your hair blonde but you've got black eyebrows, you might want to dye them too – but it's up to you.

TEDDY BOBBS ADVISES

Now gerrils, I don't want you to be putting yer hand in yer pocket too often, so here's a little tip from myself. When you see someone with nice brows, up you go to them and ask where they got them done. Gotta be smart in this game. Go to their brow merchant and get them done once in a proper shape. And then just keep them like that yourself with a tweezers.

Brows Get Groomed

There is no end of products to groom those brows, to fill in the gaps and to seal them in place. Some girlies swear by wax while others think clear mascara or humble Vaseline does the job just as well. Eyebrow pencils are still very popular with people with fair lashes. If you've over-plucked and have a bald patch, you can do a whole lot worse then fill in with a matte eyeshadow in the appropriate colour.

Brow Pencil

If you're in a hurry and only have time for a bit of a scribble, then check out Benefit's Instant Eyebrow Pencil. A soft formulation and handy brush make this a brillo handbag essential.

BROW KITS

Good old Estée Lauder comes up trumps with their deadly Brow Perfecting Duo. The ultimate kit for bold brows, it contains a shadow to fill in missing or sparse areas and a setting wax to complete your transformation.

Top Tip: There's no need to splash the cash if you don't want to: powder eyeshadow is just as good, and Vaseline can also be used to slick down unruly brows.

xgirl

I've been using the clear MAC one for years and couldn't be without it.

gingersnap

I like Smashbox Brow Tech in Soft Brown. Some of the others appear reddish, which looks artificial on me.

sarah

I use Diorshow Tinted Brow Gel, it's like a mascara for eyebrows. It shapes them, gives them great definition and makes them fuller.

Brow Wax

Check out Laura Mercier's brilliant Brow Definer. It might come in a tiny pot, but it's got mighty powers. Apply with a brush for sleek, smooth brows that'll stay put all day. Great for subtle definition.

Top Tip: When using a brow powder, go against the hair – you'll get it right into the roots, giving you better coverage.

THE PERFECT BROW SHAPE

A really good brow shape often incorporates waxing, plucking and trimming. If you don't go to a specialist brow bar, you might get only the wax or the plucking. Your therapist should have a good look at your face, judge your brows and ask you what shape you'd like.

Salon Manners

Like all salon treatments, your therapist should never tell you off about the state of your brows. Or your skin. Or your cellulite. This is why you're there – to get these things fixed! Therapists who feel the need to tell you how hairy/spotty/lazy you are need a good kick up the arse. Vote with your feet and don't go back.

And you should always be asked if you were happy with the treatment provided. If the therapist was rude or you don't think the salon is up to scratch, say so if you're brave enough. There's nothing worse then going home fuming (with one wonky eyebrow) and kicking yourself because you didn't say anything.

A good therapist is worth his or her weight in gold. If they've done a good job, leave a tip and make another appointment.

Waxing

Wax is a quick and efficient way to tidy up brows and is probably the easiest way for therapists to give you an eyebrow shape. That's why they will nearly always suggest this option. Your brows look clean and tidy afterwards and you can't really beat it for clearing up every little last stray.

But it's also one of the sorest.

There's no doubt about it that eyebrow waxing hurts. Think about it: this is the thinnest, most sensitive skin on your body. There's also a risk that wax here can damage the skin and possibly lead to premature wrinkling. It drags and pulls the skin around the eyes and takes off the top layer. Whatever you do, make sure your therapist knows what he or she is doing. Usually salons use the same wax for brows as they use for bikini and legs, and if they're double dipping (see Chapter 7, p. 157), you'll want to know about it, as this practice is quite frankly ewww and I wish it would stop.

So ask if your salon uses a special brow wax or a gentle wax such as Lycon. If they do, it will hurt a lot less and be much more gentle to your skin.

However, anyone who's got anything approaching a monobrow should just have it whipped off with regular waxes. Fellas shouldn't be embarrassed about this in the slightest – it's bread and butter work for therapists.

PLUCKING

You've probably been plucking your eyebrows since you were a tweeny and think you know how it's done, but bad plucking can be the ruination of many a Lovely Girl. Here's a few tips to help you on your way.

- Don't over-pluck. There's nothing worse then baldy brows. Remember, if you don't think you've plucked enough, you can always go back and tweeze another few hairs out later.
- If you're like me, you'll have a terrible tendency to pluck one eyebrow perfectly and then make a mess of the other one. I can never get my eyebrows to match – with the result that I end up looking like a half-crazed loon with one brow shorter/higher/thinner than the other at any time. So take your time. Look at your whole face in the mirror and make sure you're all balanced out.
- My sisters are so addicted to plucking that they whip out their tweezers at every opportunity – on the bus or at the dinner table, for example. They will pluck until their eyebrows bleed. So this is a tip for them, really: stop doing this.
- Due to this plucking craziness, we're well positioned in our family to advise on the best tweezers out there. We've tried 'em all. The ones with lights, motorised contraptions and every gimmicky yoke available. It's the Tweezerman. Nothing beats it (see panel).

SIMPLY THE BEST: TWEEZERMAN TWEEZERS

With their wide grip, Tweezerman are a cinch to use. The bright pink slant tweezers get out every single hair, no matter how tiny. Constantly rated on Beaut.ie as the must-have gadget (over GHDs and eyelash curlers), invest in a pair of these and you won't know yourself. They've got a lifetime guarantee too, so if they become misaligned or blunt you can send them off to get recalibrated. Pricier than most tweezers, but well worth it. You'll be plucking happily for years.

If you're a real pro, you can add a Tweezerman pointed tweezers to your arsenal. But these need a steady hand, so if you're in any doubt, go for the slant type.

Top Tip: If your tweezers get a bit blunt, gently sand the inside edge with emery paper to clean and sharpen them up.

Mary

I remember buying my Tweezerman – everyone thought I was bleedin' crazy because of the price, but once you use it there is no comparison with the normal tweezers.

Lipsandlashes

I love my Mr Mascara tweezers! The best tweezers I have had in a long while and my brows are the maintained proof of the pudding!

sparklicous

I heart The Body Shop tweezers. I have to have about six pairs at any one time 'cos they're so small I misplace them all the time. I recently tried a pointy pair from Boots, which was a complete waste of money 'cos the tip isn't properly aligned.

Snip Snip

As we get older, our brow hair (to say nothing of nose hair) gets longer. Sounds gross, I know, but it's true. So unless you want to look like one of those aul' fellas with the peaked eyebrows, you'll want to be trimming yours.

Brush your eyebrows upwards with an old mascara comb or eyebrow brush and trim off hairs that stick above the brow line. Do the same thing downwards and you should be neat and groomed. Don't go overboard, though, as you can knock out the shape.

And encourage your fella to do the same trimming and strimming. There's nothing worse then long, straggling eyebrows. Buy him a nose trimmer too in case he starts to get bushy nostrils.

Errol's girl

Hi girlies, got my eyebrows threaded this morning – it was absolutely amazing and the shape is fantastic and it didn't hurt at all. I thought it was going to hurt, but she said if you really know what you are doing then it won't, and nope, it didn't at all. Excellent, excellent – am deeeelighted and would highly recommend!

Threading

Threading is an Indian technique for getting rid of stray hair anywhere on the face, but it really comes into its own when eyebrows are shaped using this method.

A special smooth, coated thread that has been knotted and twisted is moved expertly across the skin, picking up and plucking out hairs as it passes. As little as one hair can be removed at a time, so the brow shape will be perfect. Unlike waxing, it won't leave skin sore and red.

To be honest, anyone who's had their eyebrows threaded by an expert raves about it – try it as soon as you can. Make sure you go to someone who's been specially trained, though, as not just anyone can do this successfully.

Kalyani

As a British-Indian lady living in Ireland for the last six years, I am just delighted to have come across this website and people who are genuinely interested in discovering the ancient art of threading. When I first came here six years ago, I was met with looks of bewilderment whenever I asked leading salons in the Dublin area whether they offered threading. They simply did not know what it was. 'No, it is not like flossing.'

Threading is not simply a beauty treatment or procedure – it is an art. That in itself should not be underestimated. I would not get my hair cut by a sheep shearer or my legs waxed by a plasterer. Not even a good plasterer.

Threading for me is like the acid test of the beauty business – get it wrong and you clearly don't understand the aesthetic of the human face. And if you don't understand that, well, I am not letting you near my nether regions for that bikini wax.

13

Eye Carumba

THE REASON WHY SOME EYESHADOWS SIMPLY BURST WITH COLOUR AND VIBRANCE IS THAT THEY'RE VERY HIGH IN PIGMENT...

Fab Colour

The reason why some eyeshadows simply burst with colour and vibrance is that they're very high in pigment. That's exactly why that set your auntie got you for Christmas – the one with the 5,000 crappy eyeshadows – doesn't last, because those shadows are made from talc and not a whole lot more. Anything bearing the dreaded hallmark of Constance Carroll or available to buy in the euro shop is best avoided.

MAC is just the business for colour choice. They've got more shades and formulations than you can shake a stick at and their eyeshadows are intense and have great staying power too. Keep an eye out for their super-frequent limited edition collections, as they're a great way to build a shadow wardrobe full of great, hard-to-find shades. There's a reason that the MAC shop in Dublin Airport is one of the busiest in the world – girls in the know flock there to snap up fabulous make-up.

I Smashbox Trios

I'm a big fan of Smashbox and the fact that it's so easily available nationwide is brill for Beaut.ies outside the capital. In particular, the brand's shadow duos and trios are fab – lots of pigment, soft textures and complementary shades make them make-up bag must-haves.

Pretty Palettes

Palettes are brilliant for the simple reason that they make everything easy-peasy lemon-squeezy. The shades that you probably bought the palette for will be there, plus others that you might not have thought of. Base shades, plus the equally important contouring and highlighting ones, are all there for you to play with. Of course there will be some horrid colours that you wouldn't put on your face in a million years, but that's the way the cookie crumbles. This has led me to having built up a collection of rakes of palettes over the years that I can't throw out because I love just one colour.

Customised Palette

Designed specifically for the gal who's never going to use that banana yellow shadow in any other offering, Bobbi Brown's Custom Palette system is the business. Buy a three, four or six-pan palette and choose the exact shades of cheek, eye and lip colours you want. While it's a bit pricey, the pans are large and you'll get *loads* of wear out of it.

FINGER ON THE PULSE: URBAN DECAY

Good old Urban Decay always come up trumps for cute palettes. With great textures and shades, their shadows are longwearing, their lip colours are bright and fun, and getting a present of an Urban Decay themed palette is A Very Nice Thing indeed.

Hey Good Looking – Benefit, I'm Talking To You

Let's not kid ourselves. While we all love make-up that performs, it's a pretty big bonus when it looks swish too. So the prize for good looks goes to Benefit. While I sometimes wish they'd make their palettes in a more robust material – cardboard isn't that handbag friendly – there's no doubt they're adorable looking.

Best of the Rest

Since Clarins redesigned their make-up range, I've been increasingly impressed with their lovely quad shadows. Make Up For Ever is a good choice for a gal who's aiming for a pro finish, Guerlain makes the ultimate in covetable luxe offerings and MAC is hard to beat for clever limited editions in stylish packaging.

AISLING'S PICK: Dianne Brill

I just can't resist Dianne Brill's flirty and fun eyeshadow trios. The colours are gorgeous and they look like very pretty matchboxes. They're so cute – and slightly naughty too. With shades like Bedroom Eyes, Naked Eyes and Candlelight Eyes, it's a dead-cert they're meant for seduction.

PRIME THE PEEPERS

What would you be doin' using an eyeshadow primer? If you've got dry skin, then you probably don't need one, but if you're a wee bit oil prone and you feel that your shadow is settling into the creases of your eyes a little too readily, then it might be time to give one a whirl. Plus, they do something else that's pretty handy, too: primer grips onto shadow and can help intensify the pigment in it. Bonus!

Urban Decay Primer Potion is a heavy-duty fixer that'll lock your eyeshadow to your lids all night long. It's also great for anchoring glitter and shimmer shadows too, meaning you won't be picking it off your *guna* the next day. Ah go on, we've all been there.

Deadly for daytime, Benefit's Lemon-Aid corrects redness and uneven skin tone, so if you're having a no make-up day, it's a quick cheat to bright eyes. It helps shadow and liner stay in place too, making it the best one I've used for the daytime.

HOW TO DO A SMOKEY EYE

Without a doubt, the smokey eye is the most-requested 'how to' on Beaut.ie. And it's no wonder – getting this wrong is oh-so-easy. Who hasn't attempted this look and ended up looking like they've been assaulted by Alice Cooper? Oh, OK, maybe that was just me, so. But sure, how do you get it right though? I turned to my sister Kirstie for advice 'cos she always gets it right. Here's her five-step guide to the ultimate smokey eye.

What you'll need:

- Two make-up brushes – one for applying shadow and the other for blending.
- A neutral base colour plus an eyeshadow duo in dark, seductive shades – I like navy, deep chocolate brown, charcoal and graphite shades for a smokin' smokey eye.
- A soft eyeliner pencil in a matching shade.
- Lashings and lashings of high-impact, vavavoom mascara.

STEP ONE: **Prep Steps**

It's all in the preparation, ladies. Apply your foundation, concealer and powder, then cover the entire eyelid in your neutral shadow shade.

STEP TWO: **Line of Your Life**

Next up, line above and below the eyes with your eyeliner pencil, using a thicker line above than below. Why? 'Cos this gives the shadow a key to grip to and will help to hold it in place all night. Once you've done that, smudge it out a little using your pinkie finger or a Q-Tip.

STEP THREE: **Application Assistance**

Apply the paler of your dark shadow shades right up to the crease of the eye – if you're not sure where that us, it's the part of the eye to the top of the eyeball and before the brow bone begins. Apply a little under the eye too, and then blend, blend, blend with your blending brush for a smooth finish. Line inside the bottom rim of the eye with your pencil liner, and set it with a little eyeshadow.

THE **BEAUT.IE** GUIDE TO GORGEOUS

STEP FOUR: Embellishment

At the outer corner of the eye, apply your darker smokey shade and blend it in well. Step back and take a good look at yourself. Need a little more definition? Add some more shadow and blend until you're happy with the result. Fancy ramping up the look a little? Add a little glitter or sparkles at this stage for an eye-popping night-time look.

STEP FIVE: Lash Back

Lastly, the ultimate eye-opening weapon we all need in our make-up arsenal: mascara. Choose one that's inky-black, volumising and lengthening and apply at least three coats for maximum glam.

Go for Glitter

Glittery shadow is a joy that everyone should experience. And I mean you here. Even if you normally only stick to subtle make-up, give this a go for a night out. It's so much fun! Start off with a little dab on the inner corner of your eye (see top tip below), and if you can rock that, you might like to go further the next time. I love MAC's Pigment pots and Faces Cosmetics' Glitter Angel Dust, as well as more purse-friendly options like Barry M's Dazzle Dust, which comes in millions of fabilis colours.

Top Tip: To add instant vavavoom to your look, put a dab of super-vibrant shadow in a contrasting shade to your main colour right in the corner of your eye. If you're using brown eyeshadow, try adding a dab of turquoise blue. If you've got lilac or purple tones as your main shade, try a green glitter. It looks fantastic – trust me!

Beware of Blue

Blue is a very difficult colour to wear on the eyes. I can't do it at all – although I'd love to. Probably your best option if you're like me and are desperate to wear blue is to opt for blue eyeliner and mascara or a touch of vibrant blue at the corners of your eyes. A very dark, midnight blue will often work too if you can't pull off paler shades.

I remember getting made up for my friend's wedding. The bridesmaids' dresses were a bluey colour and the make-up artist was insisting that everyone have blue eyeshadow, 'to match'. 'To match?' I said. 'Blue eyeshadow doesn't suit me – will you just do brown?'

'Brown?' she said with a superior smirk, wielding a dangerous-looking mascara wand mere millimetres from my eye. 'How do you think that will go with the dress then?'

'I didn't know eyeshadow had been matched to dresses since the Eighties,' I said. You can imagine how nicely she did my make-up after that.

LOVELY LINER

A huge fan of liquid eyeliner, I've tried everything from the cat's eye flick to the super thick. It's amazing what a bit of eyeliner can do for the eyes – not only does it provide instant definition round the lash line, making your god-given lashes look more abundant than they are, but applied properly, liner can make your eyes look bigger too. Sing hosannas for this truly transformative beauty product! All you need is a steady hand, a decent brush and Bob's your uncle.

And practice most definitely makes perfect here. Don't worry if you don't get it right the first (or tenth) time round – none of us did. And definitely don't attempt this after a glass or two of vino.

Best Gel Liner

Hands-down, Bobbi Brown's Long-Wear Gel Eyeliners are the pick of the liner crop. Great, inky shades, a fab texture and sheer staying power ensures we're never, ever without a pot of Sapphire Shimmer (a deep Prussian blue) in our make-up bags.

My First Eyeliner: Ruby and Millie i-writer

Easy-peasy lemon-squeezy. Give the top a couple of clicks and start drawing. Black liner is contained within a clever wand, topped by an easy-to-use brush. It's a cinch – you'll be rivaling Amy Winehouse in no time.

I also can't break my attachment to Lancôme Artliner. I've used this since my college days and it's still a staple in my make-up bag.

Colour Liner

If it's colour you want, you just have to check out the Liquidlast Liner range from MAC. Over a dozen vivid colours deliver a sharp graphic line with a great, high-shine finish. Coola Bulla.

Brush Up

Use a decent liner brush. Spend a bit on this if you can, because you'll get a better result with a pro tool. Kirstie reckons Smashbox's Arched Liner Brush #21 and MAC's 209 Eyeliner Brush are up to the job.

Great Budget Buy

Available in six shades, Rimmel's Glam'eyes Liquid liners are a good product at a great price.

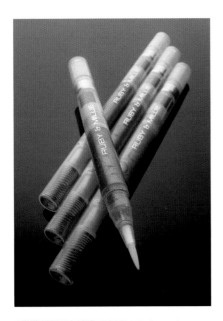

cailín
The Smashbox rigid eyeliner brush is fab, especially for use with gel eyeliner!

Jen
Bourjois Liner Clubbing liquid liner is very easy to apply. I was a liquid liner virgin until this (well, bar one awful experiment which resulted in me looking like a draggier Amy Winehouse) and it is so easy to do and get straight. They also do purty colours.

Down the Kohl Mines

There's nothing worse than getting your new eyeliner home, uncapping it and then discovering it appears to be made of a substance akin to concrete. Hate that. Dragging a stiff, solid pencil across the delicate eye area is a definite no-no, so what you want is something soft and buttery to add definition without tugging at the skin. Ouch.

Hands down, Giorgio Armani's Smooth Silk eyeliners are the best I've ever tried. Expensive, yes, but if you're a liner junkie, they're worth it. So smooth, they glide on comfortably, stay all day and are deadly for the first steps in a smokey eye, too.

Bourjois Pencils Rock

Kohl & Contour, Glitter and Metallic eye pencils from Bourjois all get our thumbs-up. Soft formulas and funky colour choices make these pencils brilliant budget buys.

baby in a corner
Elizabeth Arden Smoky Eyes eyeliner in Espresso is absolutely brilliant! Love it! Great dark colour that looks great with blue eyes!

Littlesis
I discovered that MAC Teddy is by no means a simple, one-dimensional brown eyeliner. It boasts specks of shimmer which seem to bring out the colour in my eyes, without appearing unkind to my almost transparent skin. Teddy also features a level of flexibility one would think impossible for brown eyeliner … good with browns, greys and greens! For an everyday look, this eyeliner ticks all the boxes!

Atomic_Blonde
I wear dark brown eyeliner to work and black at weekends. Currently using a Dior brown eyeliner, lovely and creamy.

Poppins
Been using MAC Teddy for four years. I adore it. I am never without it – Powersurge is also lovely lighter shade than Teddy, it's a golden brown.

SHADOW-TO-LINER MAGIC

Did you know it's a cinch to turn eyeshadow into liquid liner? Yup – no need to shell out for separate liners if you've got the exact shade you want in your collection already. Pick up a bottle of Benefit's She Laq, a liquid wonder that you can use to set make-up with, and mix with eyeshadow to create brightly coloured liquid liner.

But if that's a bit too much like DIY for you, then check out Too Faced's clever Shadow Insurance. It can be used as a primer or mixed with loose powder shadow and pigments to create smooth, cream eye liner.

laineyg

I've got the MAC Technakohl in Photogravure for 'not quite black' moments, but I'm still a bit addicted to Graphblack and black mascara that as a paler-than-pale blonde I probably shouldn't wear. I've also got a Clinique cream liner in a sort of grey-black that definitely suits better than black for day.

Bee

Gotta say, I keep returning to Lancôme Bi-Facial for make-up removal. I know it's for eyes, but I use the other side of the cotton pad for the rest of the face.

EYE MAKE-UP REMOVER

Don't forget to take all yer eye make-up back off! Wipes won't cut the mustard here, especially with sparkles, glitter and smokey eyes, so invest in a good eye make-up remover. I rate Clinique Take the Day Off and Lancôme Bi-Facial. Both are oil based and will lift even the most stubborn of slap.

Get Down with Guyliner

Manscara and guyliner? Em, just about as likely to become a trend among the majority of Irish men as pigs are to fly. Can you honestly imagine it? I'd like nothing better than to see Irish guys bothering with their appearance a bit more, but seeing as most of them are still too embarrassed to admit to the presence of 'aftershave balm' (i.e. moisturiser) in the bathroom cabinet, I think we'll be waiting a bit longer for this.

MAMMY SAYS

In the name of all that's holy, stop talking about this stupid nonsense now of men wearing make-up or I'll leather ya.

14

Gorgeous Gob

...THINGS YOU CAN DO AT HOME THAT SIMPLY AND EFFECTIVELY GIVE YOU A
BRIGHTER SMILE....

mericans laugh at the colour of Irish teeth. Yes, OK, they might have been stained a bit brown by mugs of strong tea in the past, but we're brightening them up now. And I've seen quite a few toothless mouths on 'sophisticated' shows like Jerry Springer to know that the American dream of a full set of gnashers does not exist in certain areas … Ours may be a bit crooked sometimes, but at least we usually have a full set!

QUICK TEETH FIXES

There are loads of newfangled (and expensive) treatments out there for teeth these days – veneers, bleaching, laser whitening and Invisalign braces are all popular with people looking to improve the look of their gnashers. But we're going to concentrate on things you can do at home that simply and effectively give you a brighter smile.

Crest Whitestrips

A few years ago I had one of my obsessions, about teeth this time. I went to the dentist and asked about getting them professionally whitened.

She hummed and hawed. 'Mmmm, I don't agree with this fad of getting teeth whitened, it's so American. And anyway, teeth discolouring is just part of the ageing process, it's normal.' I was speechless. Allow the ageing process to develop as normal?

I persisted. 'But that's why people dye their hair and use anti-wrinkle creams – to look younger! Why should your teeth give the game away?'

Reluctantly, she gave me an alternative tip. Apparently Crest Whitestrips Premium give similar results to professional whitening, if used correctly. And for a fraction of the price, they were pretty impressive, she thought. But you couldn't buy them in Europe, she warned, they hadn't been approved here yet. I could get them in New York when I was there next month.

I wanted them NOW, though!

I went straight home and bought them on the internet and they arrived a few days later. Like little clear pieces of clingfilm covered in slimy gel, you stick them on your teeth for 30 minutes a day for two weeks.

And the results? Yes, my teeth were considerably whitened and brightened. Not white-white or anything, but the improvement was clear.

If you want to get your teeth whitened, try the Whitestrips first. They're very pocket friendly, whereas professional whitening is definitely a credit union job.

that girl

I'm currently in New York and stocking up on this stuff – the CVS Pharmacy group here does a generic version which is almost indistinguishable from Crest Whitestripes (packaging is nearly identical as well) for a few dollars cheaper, so whiter than white teeth for moi … I shelled out the cash to have my teeth professionally whitened two years ago and was really disappointed with how quickly it faded (a few months). I think the DIY method is the best.

BLUE LIPGLOSS

It's a Beauty Rule that cool, bright shades of lipstick make your teeth look whiter. Unfortunately this means that the reverse is also true, so avoid lilac lipstick like the plague – unless you like looking like a yellow-toothed crone. But the good news is that a blue lipgloss can instantly transform less-than-ivory gnashers into pearly whites. But do they make you look like a mad robot from the future? Not a bit of it. On lips, you can't see any blue at all, just a glossy pucker and sparkling teeth.

Sharon
Diorkiss have one called Mint Lemonade. It only looks blue in the tube but it's clear on, and I don't know if it's in my head, but I do actually think my teeth look slightly whiter when it's on.

The one to try is Benefit's California Kissin'. It's a mint-flavoured lip treat that can be worn on its own or under lipstick to brighten and whiten your smile. On a cheaper note, I like Bourjois's Gloss Menthol, which whitens teeth and helps to give the impression of fresh breath because it's minty smelling. But of course it won't work if you've just been eating onions.

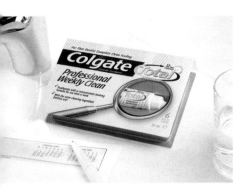

Colgate Total Professional Weekly Clean Toothpaste

This is a brilliant buy to super-clean your teeth in between dentist visits.

'Carpe Dente: seize the teeth,' said Mrs Doubtfire, fishing her falsies drunkenly out of her Chardonnay.

Now I don't have false teeth or anything, but I wanted to give my real ones a little treat. I love the feeling you get after a tooth clean by the dentist. Teeth feel so sparkly and smooth. I was a bit doubtful that the Colgate Professional Weekly Clean could give the same feeling, but sure, no harm to give it a go.

Using the same ingredients that dentists use to clean your teeth, this concentrated toothpaste promises to give you the same super-clean, run your tongue over your toothies a hundred times feeling. It can't and shouldn't be used to replace your regular dentist cleaning, though.

And does it work? Yes it does!

Use it once a week, brushing for three minutes, for results you'll see immediately. Your teeth will look whiter too, due to the hydrated silica and perlite in the toothpaste. Ahhh, instant gratification. Now that's what I like!

Kirstie
It's like a dentist scale and polish, so your teeth feel great – really clean!

CarolineJ
I've used it and my teeth felt cleaner. I asked my dentist about it and he said he had no problem with the product.

Beth
I use this and it is fabulous! I use it in conjunction with Pearl Drops Hollywood Smile (which does also work to leave super clean and white teeth).

Don't Forget

No amount of Crest Whitestrips, blue lipgloss and Pearl Drops are any substitute for regular trips to the dentist. You should aim to go twice a year for check-ups and teeth cleaning. Your PRSI payments can help out with this – just ask your dentist to see if you're eligible.

PUCKER UP

Now that we've tackled a few quick cheats to terrific teeth, it's time to turn our attention to the fun stuff: make-up. This is the bit I like the most, and in every bag and coat I own lurks a collection of glosses, balms and lipsticks that I rediscover each time I take them out of the wardrobe. They're like the gift that keeps on giving! No girl can have too many of these – don't ever feel guilty for buying yet another.

LIP BALM

One of the joys of winter is slathering on lots of lip balm. Yummy! However, a warning: the use of lip balm can easily spill over into addiction. With lots of conflicting advice around telling us that overuse can actually lead to drier lips, it's easy to be puzzled as to whether you should use it or not. I say: if you like lip balm, then it's a purse-friendly habit, and as well as being soft and moisturising, it's an instant pick-me-up. Go for it. There are much worse addictions to have.

And if you're seriously worried, we can set up a branch of Lip Balm Anonymous complete with twelve steps to wean you off. Such resources do exist on the Internet – proving that some people just have too much time on their hands. Sigh.

Top Tip: try to buy a balm with an SPF – our poor auld lips are just as subject to sun damage as the rest of our skin.

Brilliant All-rounder

So much loved I can't go any further here without mentioning Elizabeth Arden's Eight Hour Cream. It was originally developed for horses and it does smell a bit sharp – but it's a true cult buy with zillions of uses. (There are also tinted treatment lipsticks in the range, but the good auld balm is a winner for lips too).

A tiny bit provides relief for even the most chapped pout, and you can use it for so many other things too – grazes, cuticles, flaky patches of skin and even eyebrows can be tamed with it. Plus a tube of this stuff just lasts and lasts. And then lasts some more.

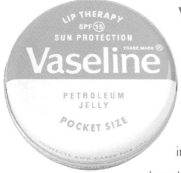

Vaseline

Vaseline is a staple in many handbags and bathroom cabinets. A bit like Eight Hour Cream, it has proved its worth down through generations of women and is also a cult beauty purchase for a reason. Most of us were introduced to Vaseline from the minute we were in nappies and have been relying on it ever since. Though hopefully you don't have nappy rash now. And if you do? Well, needless to say you have some kind of fetish and this book is not qualified to discuss it.

Little tins of Vaseline are dead cheap and come in green (with aloe vera), yellow (with SPF), pink (with rose and almond) as well as the regular blue, so just like Quality Street – there's one that's everyone's favourite. A caveat: petroleum jelly does not suit everyone, so if you find that your lips are still dry even after lashing on the Vaseline, it's probably best to stick to a specially formulated lip balm.

SJP's Mole
At this very moment I have in my handbag Elizabeth Arden Eight Hour lip balm, Carmex Click Stick, Body Shop in Passionberry, and Palmer's Cocoa Butter Lip Balm. Yeah, I think carrying around four is probably a little excessive.

Beeswax Balm

I love balms made from beeswax because they're so conditioning, and the one I'm liking the most recently is Yes to Carrots C Me Smile Lip Butters. Lovely and cheap, they come in five flavours.

PRODUCT OF YORE: Body Shop Lip Balm

Remember the obsession the teenage girls of Ireland had with Body Shop lip balm? Oh yes, you were no one unless you had a little glass pot of this stuff in your pencil case. Popular flavours included strawberry and peach. And kiwi. Hmmm – they discontinued that one, I notice.

Scrub Up

Just like skin, lips need exfoliation sometimes too, especially in winter when they're out there in freezing rain and cold. If you're finding that you have loose skin you'd like to be shot of, you can try a couple of things. One is to gently brush lips with a clean, soft toothbrush, and the other is to try a dedicated lip-exfoliating product. I like Clarins Lip & Contour Gentle Exfoliator, which tastes of raspberries and scrubs up skin in jiffy.

Top Tip: Mix a bit of sugar in with some balm for a home-made exfoliator that will slough off dead skin as it moisturises. Handy – and cheap!

Lipliner

A handy thing to have knocking about the place, there's a right way to use lipliner – which of course means there's a totally wrong way, too. That would be lining waaaay outside your natural lip line or by using a shade that clashes completely with your lipstick or gloss. You can buy special clear liner from the Body Shop – look for Lip Line Fixer. It's a waxy pencil that prevents lipstick from bleeding, without you having to worry about matching up shades.

Otherwise, it's always good to have a neutral lip pencil to hand. Everyone raves about MAC's famous Spice pencil, but I find it too dark. Give No. 7's Perfect Lips Liner in Melon a whirl instead – it's a nice warm beige. And if you're a fan of scarlet lips, then invest in one good red. I like Guerlain's Lip Pencils. Firm and easy to use, they come with a foam tip for easy smudging.

Top Tip: Make gloss last longer by colouring in your lips with liner in the same colour. That way, even if you're eating or drinking, you maintain some colour until you can nip to the ladies to top up.

AISLING'S PICK: Rimmel Lip Liner

Yes, good old Rimmel – I've never come across a better lipliner, and if you wear lipstick or gloss every day you sure do get through them. This is an absolute winner.

Lipstick

A bit out of favour there for a few years, lipstick is back with a bang. These days, it's not just for mammies. Gone are unflattering textures and yuck shades, and in are new hybrid formulations that behave like gloss but last longer, as well as long-wear products that turn your kisser into the Gobi Desert – so we won't be recommending any of those.

There's more choice than ever before too, and with matte, semi-matte, high-shine and full opaque varieties on offer, sure you'd be gone astray with the worry trying to work out what's what. So I've worked it all out for you. Ah, I know I'm very good to you.

Glossy Shine

Dior's Addict High Shine range is the one to go for if you're in a transitional stage back to lipstick from gloss. Bright yet sheer shades and lovely packaging will convert you to bullets of colour in no time.

Creamy Shine

Oh, I adore Yves Saint Laurent's amazing Rouge Volupté range. With gorgeous shades, lovely coverage that's full but creamy and luxury looks, you'll have your gal-pals clamouring to copy you.

Daytime

Both Bobbi Brown and Estée Lauder are hard to beat for lip ranges for day. In particular, check out Bobbi's Creamy Lip Colour line, a suite of moisturising neutrals that are great for the office, and Estée's Signature lipsticks in their classic gold fluted tubes.

Lip Tint

An important one, tints aren't to be overlooked and are great for staying power and for the gal who finds gloss too gloopy and lippy too old-fashioned. Bourjois's Rouge Hi-Tech range is fab for a stain that stays put.

Stay in Fashion

Yes, MAC wins again here. If you're looking to ape a catwalk trend and you're not a normal lipstick-wearer, then head straight to MAC, who is always ahead of the colour curve. Whatever's in fashion, you can guarantee MAC will have it.

Yummy and Moisturising

It's a truth often acknowledged that lipstick can leave you reaching for the balm to sort out a parched pout. If that's something you hate, then take a

zee
I have dark hair and pale skin and often wear a bright red matte-finish lipstick by MAC called Ruby Woo. It's not for the faint at heart, but it is such good fun to wear!

Kirstie
I've a Chantecaille burgundy/red which I love and which looks great patted on, as opposed to the full lip liner/brush monty.

LipGloss Bitch
Oh, I just love the The Balm lipsticks – Smut is a great colour.

Eimear
I love MAC lipsticks … have never worn anything else. Blankety is my favourite.

Jellytots

I used to wear the Heather Shimmer lipstick and that lilac eyeshadow, both from Rimmel – wouldn't leave the house without them on, so cringe-worthy!

look at Elizabeth Arden Color Intrigue Effects lipstick, which contains vitamins and lots of lovely hydrating goodness.

Top Tip: Scared of full coverage and dark lipstick shades? Pat on your colour of choice with fingers for a modern, less-defined finish.

TRICKS OF THE TRADE

We're forever being asked, 'How do I get my lipstick to stay on?' Everyone wants to get in on the secret of gloss that'll stay put all day, but I'm sorry to tell you but there's no hidden trick. Nope, the trick is preparation and constant reapplication, so line lips with a pencil in a matching shade and bring your gloss or lipstick out with you, and nip into the loo when you feel a bit lacking.

PRODUCT OF YORE:
Rimmel Black Cherry

Remember Rimmel's Black Cherry? A generation of women wouldn't leave the house without its purpley shininess smeared across their lips. But did you know that while it has (understandably) experienced a dip in popularity in recent years, it's still around? Uh huh – and at a Rimmel stand near you.

Lady in Red

The perfect shade of scarlet that's just right for you is a conundrum that shows no sign of ever abating. Red lipstick is difficult to get right, and because it's such a vibrant colour, it can be tricky to wear with confidence.

Go to a few make-up counters, check out the testers and buy a couple of cheapie lipsticks in a couple of different shades of red if you want to see which tone will suit you. Here's a few general tips.

- Don't do much eye make-up with red lipstick. A slick of eyeliner and mascara should be all that's going on, otherwise you'll look like the original painted hoor.
- If you're the classic Irish *cailín* with dark hair and pale skin, you can try a rich, ruby red. Guerlain's KissKiss Lipstick in Exces De Rouge would be only gorgeous.
- Pale-skinned blondes like Gywneth Paltrow can pull off that true-bluey red shade. Try YSL's Rouge Volupté in Red Muse.
- If you've got a sallow skin tone, try a red with a good bit of brown in it. Bobbi Brown Lip Colour in Burnt Red is ideal.
- Redheads with pale skin also suit browny-reds, but if you're a redhead with a bit more colour in your cheeks, try a pinky shade on lips, like Estée Lauder's All Day Lipstick in Rosewood.
- If you've a dark complexion, you can carry bold shades really well – look for deep cranberry and plum shades. Shocking brights will work really well too. Try Lipstick Queen's pigment-rich Sinner lipsticks in Plum Sinner and Red Sinner (from Space NK).
- Make sure you line lips to prevent the dreaded 'bleed' (lipstick migrating outside the lip line).
- Check teeth in a mirror after applying – for some reason, red lipstick seems to have a terrible habit of appearing there.

glittertastic

Packed full of lovely sparkly bits, I adore Yves Saint Laurent's Touche Brilliance range. Gleaming, glam party shades in pretty wands, sure what's not to like? A couple of clicks and apply over lipstick or on its own for shimmery, glimmery luscious lips. A mothers-of-pearl extract is one of the ingredients that make this gloss so radiant. And like all of YSL's make-up, it smells gorgeous too.

MontyC

I've bought loads of these lip glosses and I absolutely love 'em! Love the colours and the sparkle is just right (for me anyway) .

Penny Century

I love Clinique's Superbalm lip gloss – the colours are lovely and it's not as gloopy as, say, Juicy Tubes.

You're probably sick to the back teeth of magazines telling you that everyone can wear red lippie. Fact is, they can't, because it simply won't suit some people. So don't worry if you can't – pinky or browny lipsticks are much more flattering and easier to wear, so step away from the red if it's really not working for you.

GLOSS

Arguably most women's lip-slick of choice, gloss has been huge in beauty for what seems like forever. It's brilliant stuff, really – there's no worries about going outside the lines, you can pretty much apply it anywhere and it can take you from day to night in an instant. Be warned – wind, long hair and gloss do not mix, unless, of course, you enjoy picking your highlights out of your mouth every two seconds. But on the plus side, gloss is glam, flirty and a brilliant choice for anyone with less-than-generous lips.

Like everything in life, not all glosses were created equal. Here's what I rate.

Grown-up Glam

Not quite as vavavoom as other offerings, Chanel's Lèvres Scintillantes glosses are perfect for the more sophisticated gal among us. Available in literally millins of shades, there's one for everyone, from pale nudes through to pinks and reds.

AISLING'S PICK: DiorKiss

Squeezy, gorgeous, shiny, yum! The clear Sorbet Meringue shade works with every look.

Nudies

Nude lip gloss is a great fall-back to have in the make-up bag. If you're wearing dramatic eye make-up or just want a natural look, check out the Bourjois Effet 3D Nudes trio of glosses, which are shiny, tawny and super-flattering.

Plump up the Volume

I can't say I'm a mad fan of lip-plumping glosses, as they often contain stingy ingredients like chilli to irritate lips so that they literally swell up. The effect is only temporary, but sure, if you like that sort of thing, then give them a go for special occasions. DuWop's Lip Venom and Urban Decay's Big Fatty Lip Plumper are two that get the thumbs-up time and time again.

One that's a bit kinder to your lips is Rimmel's Volume Booster Lip Gloss, which uses hyaluronic acid (steady, it's not dangerous) to add extra hydration and moisture to the skin on the lips, making them look fuller.

SJP's Mole

Bourjois 3D Effet: smells like Love Hearts sweets and is quite balm-like. I even wore one on my wedding day – Rose Emblématic, which is this lovely champagne rose. My mother STILL goes on about how pretty the shade was! The one on my desk is Rose Arctic, which is a more nude-y rose and great for work.

Tiddles

Stila Lip Glazes are gorge – and taste delish too! I had a reddish one when I was a teen and used to just eat it off my lips. Yummers.

Siobhan

MAC Cushy White is my favourite. It has the added benefit of lip plumpers as well. I mix it with nude lip liner.

Faking It: A Top Trick for the Perfect Pout

To make your bottom lip look bigger, paint over your natural lip line ever so slightly with lipstick. Then go around the area with a pale concealer directly – it has the effect of faking the natural lip line. This works, I promise!

Stockists

A

- **Annick Goutal**, at House of Fraser, Dundrum
- **APIVITA**, at pharmacies nationwide
- **Armani, Giorgio Cosmetics**, at Brown Thomas Dublin and Cork, and Dublin Airport
- **Aveda**, at Brown Thomas Dublin and Cork, House of Fraser and Whetstone salons

B

- **Benefit**, at department stores nationwide and from www.benefitcosmetics.com
- **Barry M**, at Superdrug stores and selected Boots, and direct from www.barrym.com
- **Betty Beauty**, at Cristalle Beauty & Day Spa, Mayo 096 77391 and from www.bettybeauty.com
- **Biotherm**, at DAA Travel Value Airport Shopping
- **Bliss**, at Brown Thomas Dublin, Cork and Limerick, and Harvey Nichols, Dundrum and from www.strawberrynet.com
- **Bobbi Brown**, at Brown Thomas Dublin, Cork and Galway
- **Body Shop**, at stores nationwide
- **Bourjois**, at pharmacies nationwide
- **Brown Thomas**, Dublin, Cork, Limerick and Galway and from www.brownthomas.com
- **Bumble and Bumble**, www.bumbleandbumble.com

C

- **Cetaphil**, at pharmacies nationwide
- **Chanel**, at department stores and good pharmacies, 01 463 7379
- **Chantecaille**, at Nue Blue Eriu, Dublin
- **Clarins**, at pharmacies and department stores, 01 284 6477
- **Clerys**, 18–27 Lower O'Connell Street, Dublin 1, 01 878 6000
- **Clinique**, at department stores nationwide
- **Crème de la Mer**, at Brown Thomas Dublin, Cork and Galway

D

- **Dr. Hauschka**, at Clerys, Nelsons Homeopathic Dispensary and health food stores nationwide, 01 289 6990, and at Brown Thomas Dublin
- **Dr LeWinns**, at Arnotts
- **Dr Sebagh**, at Brown Thomas Dublin
- **Danné**, at salons, 01 286 4770
- **Darphin**, at Arnotts
- **Decléor**, at salons
- **Dermalogica**, at salons nationwide, 1850 556785, and from www.awin1.com
- **Dianne Brill**, at Nue Blue Eriu
- **Dior Cosmetics**, at department stores
- **Diptyque**, at Brown Thomas
- **Dove**, at supermarkets and pharmacies
- **Doux Me**, at Nue Blue Eriu

E

- **Egypt Wonder**, at leading pharmacies, Arnotts, Clerys and Shaws
- **Elemis**, at spas nationwide, 0044 127 872 7830
- **Elizabeth Arden**, at department stores nationwide

E

- **Eminence Organics**, at Anne McDevitt, Wicklow Street, Dublin and Castle Leslie Spa, Glaslough, Co. Monaghan
- **Essie**, at selected salons nationwide
- **Estée Lauder**, at department stores nationwide
- **Eucerin**, at pharmacies nationwide
- **Eve Lom**, at Revive, Milltown, Dublin 6, 01 260 4781, and Harvey Nichols

F

- **Faces Cosmetics**, at Arnotts and Navan Shopping Centre
- **Face2**, St Martins House, Waterloo Road, Dublin 4, 01 607 7923
- **Frederic Fekkai**, at Space NK branches, Belfast, and Brown Thomas Dublin

G

- **Garnier**, at supermarkets nationwide
- **GHD**, at Peter Mark salons nationwide
- **Giorgio Armani Cosmetics**, at Brown Thomas Dublin and Cork, and Dublin Airport
- **Givenchy**, at department stores nationwide
- **Guerlain**, at Arnotts
- **Guinot**, at salons, 0818 719303

H

- H2O+, at Clerys and leading pharmacies
- Hamilton Tru Bronze, at selected pharmacies
- Harvey Nichols, Dundrum Town Centre, Dublin 16, 01 291 0488
- House of Fraser, Dundrum Town Centre, Dublin 16, 01 299 1400

I

- IsaDora, at department stores and leading pharmacies nationwide

J

- James Brown haircare, at larger Boots stores
- Jemma Kidd, at Boots
- Jessica Nails, at Queen Beauty Emporium and salons
- Jo Malone, at Brown Thomas Dublin and Cork
- Joico, at hair salons nationwide

K

- Kanebo Cosmetics, from www.strawberrynet.com
- Keraskin, at Mizu of Riverlane, Dundalk and Adore Salon, Oliver Plunkett Street, Cork
- Kérastase, at L'Oréal Professional salons, including Peter Mark branches, 01 604 5935
- Kevyn Aucoin, at Queen Beauty Emporium, see entry p. 294
- Kimberly Sayer, from www.lovelula.com
- Kimia, from www.lovelula.com
- Korres, at Harvey Nichols and Nue Blue Eriu, see entry overleaf

L

- La Prairie, at Brown Thomas Dublin and Nue Blue Eriu, see entry overleaf
- La Roche-Posay, at pharmacies nationwide
- Lancôme, at department stores and pharmacies nationwide
- Laura Mercier, at Brown Thomas Dublin, Cork, Limerick and Galway
- Lavera, at health food stores nationwide and from www.evenone.com
- Leighton Denny, at salons and www.beautydevil.ie

- Liz Earle, from www.qvcuk.com and www.lizearle.com, and Wilde & Green, Miltown, Dublin 6
- L'Occitane, stores nationwide, and from www.loccitane.com
- L'Oréal Paris, at pharmacies and supermarkets

M

- MAC, at Brown Thomas, selected BT2 stores and Dublin Airport
- Matis, 01 460 5055
- Maybelline, at pharmacies and supermarkets
- Max Benjamin, from www.vanillacotton.ie, and at Brown Thomas Dublin
- Max Factor, at pharmacies nationwide
- Menard, at Arnotts
- Model.Me, at Boots
- Models Prefer, from www.qvcuk.com
- Molton Brown, at spas, including Carton House, shops at Dundrum Town Centre, Kildare Village, 21 Wicklow Street, Dublin 2, www.qvcuk.com, and at Brown Thomas
- Murad, at Carter Beauty, Dun Laoghaire, and from www.murad.ie

N

- Nádúr Organics, at health food stores, boutiques and pharmacies nationwide, and from www.nadurorganics.ie
- Nails Inc., at Brown Thomas Dublin, Cork and Limerick and BT2 Dundrum
- NARS, at Brown Thomas Dublin
- Nelsons Homeopathic Dispensary, Duke Street, Dublin 2, and from www.nelsonshomeopathy.com
- NeoStrata, at pharmacies nationwide
- Nivea, at supermarkets nationwide
- No Scream Cream, at salons, including Akina in Temple Bar
- Nue Blue Eriu, 7 South William Street, Dublin 2, 01 672 5776 and IFSC Shopping Centre, Custom House Quay, Dublin 1, 01 636 0140
- NUXE, at larger Boots and House of Fraser

O

- OPI, at salons nationwide
- Organic Surge, Boots Liffey Valley, Clerys, Dunnes, Hickeys, McCabes, Unicare

pharmacies and independant pharmacies
nationwide

- **Origins**, at Arnotts, Clerys, House of Fraser, Boots Liffey Valley and Dublin Airport

P

- **Pantene**, at supermarkets and pharmacies
- **Paul and Joe**, at Seagreen, The Make-up Boutique, Belfast, Purity Everyday Elegance, Ballina and from www.hqhair.com
- **Peter Mark**, nationwide, and from www.petermark.ie
- **Pevonia Botanica**, at Monart Destination Spa, and the Spa at the Heritage, Co. Laois
- **PFB Vanish**, at selected pharmacies
- **Philosophy**, from www.strawberrynet.com
- **Prescriptives**, from Brown Thomas Dublin and House of Fraser, Dundrum

Q

- **Queen Beauty Emporium**, 66–67 Aungier St, Dublin 2, 01 478 9633

R

- **Redken**, at salons nationwide, 01 604 5920
- **REN**, at Clerys, Nue Blue Eriu, Alchemist Earth, or call 01 461 0645
- **Revlon**, at larger Boots stores (including Liffey Valley), Debenhams branches and independent pharmacies nationwide
- **Rimmel**, at supermarkets and pharmacies nationwide
- **RoC**, at pharmacies nationwide

S

- **Seavite**, Debenhams, pharmacies and health food stores
- **Sebastian Professional**, at salons, 1800 236 303
- **Shiseido**, at department stores, including Arnotts and Brown Thomas, 01 456 9288
- **Shu Uemura**, from www.strawberrynet.com
- **Siana**, at Aldi stores nationwide
- **Sisley**, at Brown Thomas Dublin and Cork
- **Skin Wisdom**, at Tesco stores nationwide

- **Smashbox**, at Arnotts, Clerys, Dublin Airport, House of Fraser, Dundrum and selected pharmacies nationwide
- **Soap & Glory**, at Harvey Nichols, Dundrum and larger Boots stores
- **Sothys**, at spas and salons, 01 286 4770
- **Stila**, from www.hqhair.com
- **St. Tropez**, at department stores and pharmacies nationwide

T

- **Too Faced**, at Debenhams and larger Boots stores
- **Tom Ford**, at Brown Thomas Dublin, Cork and Limerick
- **Trish McEvoy**, at Brown Thomas Dublin and Harvey Nichols

U

- **Urban Decay**, at Debenhams and larger Boots stores

V

- **Vichy**, at pharmacies nationwide
- **Vita Liberata**, at Arnotts
- **Voya**, www.voya.ie, at Avoca Stores and Alchemist Earth

W

- **Weleda**, at health food stores nationwide and from www.lovelula.com, Nelsons Homeopathic Dispensary

Y

- **Yes to Carrots**, at pharmacies and Shaws department stores, 01 286 5976
- **Yon-Ka**, at salons, 01 832 1108
- **Yves Saint Laurent**, at department stores including Brown Thomas and Arnotts, 021 463 4080

Websites

Adonis Grooming: www.awin1.com

The cheapest Dermalogica on the web (up to 50 per cent off retail prices). Need we say any more? But we will: loads of other brands, very fast shipping, free samples.

www.benefitcosmetics.com

The online shop of one of the best cosmetic companies around. Quirky, fun and above all, great products.

www.buycosmetics.com

Big choice of brands: MAC, YSL, Clinique, Decléor, Elizabeth Arden and pretty much everything in between. Often savings as big as 75–80 per cent, loads of three-for-two and buy one get one free offers, unusual brands, slimming and detox products.

www.fragrancedirect.co.uk

Oh so cheap! Perfumes and smellys, obviously, but also an expanding range of cosmetics and other wonderous bits 'n' pieces from the likes of Too Faced, Hard Candy and Urban Decay.

www.HQhair.com

Fantastic online shop with the best goodies and the best luxury ranges. The biggest choice of hair care – Kérestase, Redken, Bumble and Bumble, Terax as well as GHD specialists. Also skin care, HQman for guys, HQOutletstore, make-up, gifts. Specialises in hard-to-find ranges.

www.lovelula.com

The essential source of all things organic and additive free. We love this website! If you have sensitive skin, are vegan or just plain love gorgeous natural cosmetics, this is the place to buy Burt's Bees, Green People, Lavera, Mother Earth, Weleda and quite literally tons more paraben-free goodness.

www.strawberrynet.com

The best online shop, no question. Huge choice and huge savings across a big range of cosmetics, skin care and perfume/aftershave. All the big names, including Clinique, Lancôme, MAC, Estée Lauder, Kérastase, Bliss, Smashbox and dozens more. Free shipping. Joyously, if you do incur a duty charge on a Strawberrynet order, the delightful Kitty Wong will refund it to you. Phew!

www.qvcuk.com

If we said we were addicted, would you hold it against us? QVC only have top-quality beauty treats from the likes of Smashbox, Bare Ecsentuals, Liz Earle, Molton Brown and many more. Introductory offers, Today's Special Value, anniversary prices – and buy it all online with a no-quibble returns policy.